I0468437

12 LAWS OF SUCCESSFUL ENTREPRENEURS

GOLDEN RULES TO ACHIEVE GREATNESS IN YOUR BUSINESS

2016 Edition

MAURICIO CHAVES MESÉN

THE TIMELESS WISDOM COLLECTION

Ralph Waldo Emerson once said: *"Consider what you have in the smallest chosen library. A company of the wisest and wittiest men that could be picked out of all civil countries in a thousand years, have set in best order the results of their learning and wisdom.*

The men themselves were hid and inaccessible, solitary, impatient of interruptions, fenced by etiquette; but the thought which they did not uncover to their bosom friend is here written out in transparent words to us, the strangers of another age."

TWC is YOUR small library. Thousands of individual books and anthologies, the best of the best in fiction and non-fiction: the greatest works of the 19th and 20th Century, written by men and women whose lives were committed to enlighten the world with the wisdom of the ages.

We publish the greatest classic and modern literature... Hemingway, Faulkner, Wells, Orwell, Huxley, Doyle, Twain, Burroughs, Chesterton, C. S. Lewis, Louisa May Alcott, L. M. Montgomery, J. M. Barrie, H. Rider Haggard, Edgar Wallace, and hundreds more... Authors who have enriched our lives and forever enlarged our capacity to dream, to get enamoured by the characters, to suffer their pain and their tragedies, and to enjoy their triumphs as if they were ours; as if they were true...

For the best self-development and positive-thinking, our authors include names as Napoleon Hill, Dale Carnegie, Charles A. Haanel, William Walker Atkinson, Orison Swett Marden, Wallace Wattles, James Allen, Christian D Larson, Ernest Holmes, Ralph Waldo Trine, Elizabeth Towne, Florence Scovell-Shinn, Charles Fillmore, and many more.

In Psychology, we have the works of Sigmund Freud, Carl Jung, Emile Coué, Isador Coriat and Alfred Adler, as well as prominent philosophers like Bertrand Russell and Alfred North Whitehead. For theosophy and mysticism, our authors include Blavatsky, Bulwer, Annie Besant, William Judge, Charles Leadbeater, A. P. Sinnet,.. We have extraordinary scientist like Charles Galton Darwin, Sir Arthur Stanley Eddington and J.W.Dunne; successful industrialists that changed our modern world as Henry Ford, Andrew Carnegie and Charles Schwab; and brilliant Economists that shaped our future as John Maynard Keynes...

Thousands of masterpieces that have brilliantly captured the essence of life in its different manifestations, have been carefully selected and are now being placed in your hands. *The results of the learning and wisdom of the greatest minds, set in best order,* as Emerson would say. Books for enlightenment, learning, illumination... that will provide the seeker –the one who is ready and is paying attention–, some of the deepest answers to life.

CONTENTS

WHAT TO EXPECT FROM THIS JOURNEY.

This is a book for entrepreneurs and those who want to be, because as entrepreneur I am convinced that we are the group which is more connected to the powerful human ability to create... That is why we love inventing new things, new concepts, new businesses...

However, despite the importance of what we do, there is very little material to help us in the day to day of creating jobs and opportunities.

I don't teach here top-secret marketing techniques; or the formula to buy properties for a dollar or penny stock to sell for five dollars. What I provide are golden rules that will help you understand real business situations and how to handle them.

Being an entrepreneur is gratifying, and has many rewards. Finances, self-esteem, personal fulfillment... That's why so many choose this path. However, people forget it's not just about having a vision to create something, and then make it grow with a little luck and some intelligence... Nothing is further from the truth!

Although this is undoubtedly the most beautiful part –the part we all dream about-, we make the mistake of thinking this is all there is, and forget the other side of the equation. The other side which includes managing workers and paying them twice a month, dealing with customers, suppliers or partners, doing marketing, monitoring the competition, paying taxes... And here is where we fail!

From hot dog carts to lingerie shops; from large companies to multi-million dollar projects, all businesses face similar probabilities of success or failure. "Fifty-fifty". And if this were not enough to scare people off, another 40% closes before three years.

Less than 10% survive the three year mark, and very few are still standing after fifty years.

So, what's the problem? If dozens of books tell us what to do, why are there so many failures? What are we doing wrong? Why so many dreams get shattered? Why so many get so traumatized that they choose to remain as employees the rest of their lives? 8 to 5, steady check, right?

The answer is: the brain has two areas, one creative, and the other administrative.

Generally, entrepreneurs concentrate in creating, and neglect the other area, not understanding that they are both necessary. Once created, companies are formed and affected by human beings and human interactions, by situations that you need to learn to manage and control. Situations not taught at business schools and about which so little is written.

I have an MBA, and I can assure you that in managing my businesses, very little of what I learned there was really important.

To learn to be an entrepreneur, you need many years on the trenches, learning from success but also from failure. When everything is going well, we don't learn. And we don't learn because we believe we are doing everything right (even if it is not true).

However, when we fail... we dissect every last detail!

These 12 Laws are the *Concentrated Juice* extracted from those experiences. I make them available to you in the hope that you won't have to go through years of disappointments and failure, as I had to experience to learn them.

My story is not different to that of thousands of entrepreneurs. After getting my law degree, I worked as an attorney for the Government, while I continued with my Masters in Business. Then I worked for the World Bank and as a consultant, and then I said, ENOUGH! No more punching cards at 8 am... It's not for me. And at 28 I decided to follow my dreams.

And since in this life everything we ask in faith we receive, God gave me my first company. The problem is, I asked for the company, not the wisdom to manage it!

The following ten years became a permanent putting out of fires. Fire after fire! Behind the appearance of increasingly large and successful companies -that collectively were worth over twenty million dollars- was a story full of mistakes and lack of wisdom...

It was the story of a castle about to collapse.

Then along came the Big Recession of 2008... The water in the hydrant dried up and I could not put out any more fires... The inevitable happened. The winter arrived. The cows got skinny...

You read in books about events like these, and you think it could never happen to you. But to get caught up in the dark after a storm, is so hard. The feelings of guilt; the self-accusations of stupidity; the memories of all the people that we made rich and the employees that stole from us; the money that we did not manage well; the people to whom we couldn't fulfill the promises, the things we used to have and now were gone...

Failure is such a torture! We all know it is a learning experience; even that maybe it is the way for "the Universe" to tell us we were in the wrong path...But the truth is, when you are facing it, it is really, really hard.

However there is always, always, always! calm after a storm. Even the darker nights are followed by morning and the rising sun. And life gives us two choices.

1. To accept defeat. To accept that we are not smart enough, or not able to have businesses or being good stewards. To believe that perhaps we are not worthy of the trust that so many people put in us...

2. To learn the lessons and move on.

I read in a book by Bryan Tracy about Phil Knight, creator of Nike, one of the most important companies in the world (Nike don't just makes shoes, it creates fashion!). A regular guy not unlike you or me, who dreamed of being an entrepreneur. He tried many times, but failed again and again and again, because he could not make people believe in his idea. However, once, he hit a home run. He hit it big!

When years later someone asked him about the secret to his success, he replied: "I knew I just had to be successful one last time. Because once you're successful, all your previous failures are simply forgotten. No one remembers!"

The day I read this, a couple of tears left my eyes. I told my wife it was an onion I was peeling...

However, I understood!

I understood that instead of complaining, thinking about the mistakes, about that effort gone with the wind, I had to concentrate my energies on my next win, on my next big success. Because once I made it again, once I hit my next Home Run, those who had witnessed my storm would not even remember my dark times.

I then used my time to think, to write, and to learn. . I read Proverbs, -the best business book in the world, no matter if you are Christian, Jew, Muslim or Scientologist. I read every single motivational book I could get. I learned with those who know.

Then, without blaming myself, without calling myself a fool, without complaining every day for the "things" I used to have that were no longer there, I was determined to never repeat those mistakes again... if only I would apply the laws and truths that life had taught me.

This book is about these laws and truths. In the process of learning them, there were tears and pain. You don't have to suffer the same, though. Try this advice, and you will see your company prosper beyond your imagination.

But believe it! Really believe it!

This is a fabulous Principle. Life has a little bit (or a lot!) of *The Matrix*. If you believe something with all your heart, you will receive it. If you believe that you will be successful, you will be. *Ask and you shall receive.*

Read this book with an open mind, knowing that in the end, you will be ready to be a better entrepreneur.

I promise it will be an interesting journey.

Mauricio Chaves

DEDICATION

To my wife Marilú. We have been together for sixteen years and she has fulfilled the promise she once made: 'In good times and in bad times...'

Your invaluable advice while writing this book, your phrases and ideas, were fundamental to it.

To my daughter Maria José... Life rewarded me with you... Every single day you make me happy, you fill me with pride and even give me words of wisdom that I know, could only come from Above. I love you.

PART ONE.
Success Is A Mental State That You Can Program!

LAW #1
FIND OUT WHAT YOU REALLY WANT IN LIFE, AND MAKE A PLAN TO ACHIEVE IT.

You've got to find what you love and that is as true for work as it is for lovers. Your work is going to fill a large part of your life and the only way to be truly satisfied is to do what you believe is great work. And the only way to do great work is to love what you do. If you haven't found it yet, keep looking and don't settle. *Steve Jobs. Stanford University Commencement Address, 2005*

a. Why to become an entrepreneur?

One of the biggest challenges faced by entrepreneurs -or those who want to become entrepreneurs, is that most of them have only one thing clear. When asked why they want to do this, most will respond: **Money! I want to make more money!**

When they realize it sounds a bit inappropriate, they add things like, *"I want to be free; do what I like; have more time for myself; fulfill my dreams..."*

But the ugly truth is that what most people want is **more money!**

Obviously, I don't blame them. We live in a culture where money has become so important, that it determines where we live, with whom we interact, how *"socially"* acceptable are our activities, how people "see" us, and what do our friends comment behind our backs in parties... A culture where people **respect *the money,* not the person!**

We have learned to be defined based on the car we drive, the house we live in, the money we show; and to believe that the solution to achieve this dream **is to have a business**. Whatever business it might be!

'So, what do you do?'

'Me? I am a businessperson...' we say with a smile showing how successful we feel. *'I opened a business because I had some ideas and some capital. I'm even thinking about expanding next year...'*

We are such a success! Right?

Well, not everything that glitters is gold!

It is not just about the money. It is not about having a business, any business. That's not how it works. If that is how you approach it -just for the money, you are going to walk aimlessly, putting out fires, and hopefully, making a bit of money that you cannot even enjoy because of stress.

To achieve real success, the secret is to understand what you really want in life, and then work will all your might to get it.

I know, I know. You've heard this before. *'Do what makes you happy'*. It sounds so **New Age**...

But even though it sounds like propaganda, the ones who understand this simple truth are the ones who become successful entrepreneurs: those who define their purpose and make of fulfilling it their source of income.

b. And, what about *purpose*?

I never did a day's work in my life. It was all fun. Thomas Edison

What do Steve Jobs, Oprah Winfrey, and Thomas Edison have in common? They created empires around their purpose and dreams; around doing exactly what they liked. And in the process became billionaires!

I few years ago —just before his death— I saw Steve Jobs presenting his latest revolutionary invention, and what I saw was a child fulfilling another dream. He wasn't at that stage because he wanted more money. He just loved what he did. So, he kept doing it to the last of his forces, and with the last breaths of life his soul was still thinking, dreaming, creating, in other words, living!

The same can be said of Ophra, the world's richest show biz entrepreneur. For 25 years she changed the world of television; and in a big way, improved the perception towards African Americans (let me be bold and say that without her there would not be Barack Obama!). Her secret has been to be happy doing what she loved and fulfilling her purpose. The rest, the millions, were just a nice addition.

To be happy, fulfilled, and to achieve success and prosperity, we have to discover our talents–art, sports, science, writing, sales, and use them to accomplish our purpose regardless of what happens around.

So, what is this *purpose, vision or destiny* about?

I believe we all have a mission in the grand scheme of things; something we came to this Earth to do. To accomplish it we were given certain talents.

So, if you really want to be a successful entrepreneur, first you need to determine: Who are you? What moves you? What do you enjoy doing? It does not matter what it is, anything goes. Ultimately, it is you. Do you like to invent or build things? Do you like to cook? Are you a natural salesperson? Are you a good writer? Do you have an eye for detail? Do you have great taste decorating? Do you like sports? Are you a talented painter? Do you sing really well? Do you dance well? Do you like animals?

What makes you special? What makes you so happy you would be willing to do it without getting paid?

This first step is so important! And don't worry if what you like is rare or unique. I can guarantee you (or you can find it on you tube), that there are people being happy and making money doing things so strange that you can't imagine (as the guy who cut two holes in a sheet, made sleeves on it and called it the Snuggie; or just by singing, dancing or selling cotton candy.

"You can be who you want to be" says the famous saying. And to be *whom you want to be* will make the difference between being desperate to run out of the office or continue to work twelve hours. Between leaving everything behind when your company is in trouble, or fighting to the end.

To make a lot of money you need that extra motivation which will bring you to go the extra mile.

In this book I will try to show you how to fulfill your desire to become an entrepreneur; what to do and what not to do! I will try to be a mentor to show you the realities you will find in pursuing your dreams; so you hopefully don't have to learn these lessons the hard and painful way.

However, no matter how many lessons you memorize and learn by heart, your success will depend on finding something that makes you deeply happy.

c. Make a good plan.

I was recently called to a meeting in another city, to an address that frankly I did not know.

As I was in a hurry and didn't want to be late (and because I thought I more or less knew where I was going) I didn't program my GPS or check in any maps. I just got in the car and started driving as fast as I could.

Of course, since I didn't know where I was going... I got lost! And I ended up arriving late, even though I violated every single speed limit! However, something good came out of this experience. When I finally reached my destination, I thought of this truth:

It is not about going faster, but about knowing where you want to go. Those who reach the goal are those who start prepared, knowing exactly where they are going.

If I would have prepared the route, even if I had left five minutes later, I would have driven more relaxed, arrived early, and would have not added a millimeter to my ulcer. But since I didn't prepare, I stressed all the way, wondering what would happen if I got lost... And I couldn't think of what really mattered: What I was going to say at the meeting!

And my friends, life is like this.

So get ready! Plan your life. Draw a detailed map. Outline exactly what you want. Where exactly do you want to go? How are you going to do it? What are the steps you must take to get where you want to go?

Napoleon Hill said that one must have a *defined purpose,* and then inject it with burning desire, because only the thoughts injected with emotion can stimulate the subconscious to achieve what you want. In other words, feel it deeply; feel it in your gut. Remember that feelings are a powerful force!

Wouldn't you like to walk through life knowing that you are going somewhere?

The ability to know where you are going is paramount, because once you understand where you are going, you can develop the right character and the talents and skills that you need. If you can see your destination in the horizon, even if you fall during your journey, you will stand up, shake the dust, and continue walking, because you know what your goal, and your target, is.

Stop being a drifting boat. If God put in birds, fish, butterflies, turtles, penguins, and many other animals, the ability to find the place they were born to fulfill the sacred mission to reproduce -no matter if it is thousands of miles away, just imagine the powerful magnet inside you, longing to take you exactly where -since before you were born, you were destined to go...

The road to success begins when you take a piece of paper, and draw your path. And when you write your dreams, remember that everything in the universe is about creation and expansion. All activity is based on the desire to grow and move forward. The world is growing, creating new things every day. The universe is expanding by millions of miles, creating new planets, new galaxies... The same force creating these galaxies, the same substance, is the material used in creating your dreams and all wealth in the world. So, grow, expand! Has anyone ever lied to you and convinced you that wealth is scarce? No! Wealth is abundant; but our mistaken beliefs prevent us from acquiring or even approaching it. It is DOUBT (not accepting the universal truth that everything we believe leaving no room for doubt happens), what doesn't let us believe that money can come to us.

d. And... Action!

If you are committed to start a business; you know what you want; outlined your plan; convinced yourself you can do it; and added the *burning desire, the feelings* mentioned in so many books, it is time to take the next step:

Wake up! Awaken your talents!

Take action! Start working immediately and with enthusiasm for what you want! *"A man can succeed at almost anything for which he has unlimited enthusiasm" says Charles Schwab.*

Add commitment to the talents you have been given, so they can reach levels you can't even imagine. Your thinking is important, but your action is critical. Anything worth achieving in life requires effort. *Maybe I should have left this for later chapters. Some people, when somebody mentions work and effort...*

Although as stated earlier, when you do what you love, it does feel like fun and not like work.

What do you want? Can you see it in your mind? Can you believe it? There is a difference between wanting something and being ready to receive it. You have to believe, not just to desire. And then take action! If someone just wants and desires but does not believe or act, he is nothing but a dreamer.

If you dream of cooking, COOK! Create recipes, find new ingredients, learn new things, but cook! If you only dream about being a chef, but do nothing, the day you die your tombstone will say: *Here lies a secretary or a worker or a doctor, whose only dream was to cook, but never did anything for it.*

If you want to be a motivator, start by giving small talks. If you want to be a great singer, at least go to karaoke.

"Nothing is beneath you, if it is in the direction of your life; nothing is great or desirable if it is off from that", says Emerson in "Conduct of Life."

So, if it is in the direction of your life, who cares if it is too "small"! Even the largest tree began as a seed. Then it was a small plant. Then a bush. Then a big tree. And finally, it became the largest tree on the PLANET!

And stop believing in bad things, stop believing in doom prophecies and Nostradamus (my novels, a trilogy called Knights of Nostradamus, are about these issues. This, of course, is an ad!)

Stop believing the world is going to hell; that only bad things will happen. Stop feeding your mind with negative thoughts that do nothing but to grow in your subconscious as bad seeds, which becomes weeds and end up drowning the offspring of your dreams. Stop watching the news at eleven; and start learning about all the amazing things happening in technology, which are changing for better the world in which we live.

Don't complain; invent something! The next iPhone; the next website; the next building style; the next software to allow robots to interact with humans.

Create a Symphony, paint the next Sistine Chapel or sculpt the next David. Think of the next Snuggie; the best dog training manual; the next exercise to lose weight, or a great new recipe for a hot dog.

Stop whining and complaining, and help building a better world! The ones that do this usually become millionaires...

PRINCIPLES OF THE CHAPTER

• Do not become an entrepreneur just because you think it's the best way to make money. We all want to make money; it is an important part of life. But not everyone is willing to take the huge risks involved in starting and maintaining a business.

• If you already decided to become an entrepreneur, first determine who you are, what you enjoy doing, and what your unique and special talents are. Try to start a business or undertaking related to what makes you happy and you love to do. That will ensure that you're willing to invest the enormous personal commitment that is required, as well as to provide a lot of work and effort. The process has great rewards, but you have to be willing to pay the price. And remember that if it's something you love, time will fly, and you will enjoy every minute. Otherwise, you will probably be completely miserable in this new adventure, and at the first sign of trouble, you'll want to quit and run.

• If you have a dream, specific goals, high expectations, you know where you are going, you have identified your talents, and you know what you want, now, go for it! Do not expect your environment to change before you act; change your environment with your actions!

LAW #2.
FOCUS ON SUCCESS

There is a thinking stuff from which all things are made, and which, in its original state, permeates, penetrates, and fills the interspaces of the universe.

A thought in this substance produces the thing that is imaged by the thought.

A person can form things in his thought, and, by impressing his thought upon formless substance, can cause the thing he thinks about to be created.

In order to do this, a person must pass from the competitive to the creative mind. He must form a clear mental picture of the things he wants, and must do — with faith and purpose — all that can be done each day, doing each separate thing in an efficient manner.

Wallace Wattles, The Science of Getting Rich.

In *Think success*, my other book (which I wrote with the help of my wife and my daughter), we discuss the universal principles of motivation and the pursuit of success set out in dozens of sources. I share here some of these principles, as it is clear that to be a great entrepreneur, the first requirement is to believe in yourself and focus on success.

a. What is Success?

We all want something called *success,* but if you ask around, most people have no idea what this word means. In principle, by the standards of this society, it seems to be something measured in millions of dollars.

We have the one million club, the ten million, the hundred million, the billionaire's club... We have the 500 richest in the world, the 500 richest in the country, the five richest in town...

And if you want to go even more personal, we have the rich uncle, the rich cousin, the millionaire friend. However, true success -and his twin sister, prosperity- is not just about the money but about achieving a balance between many areas, such as:

• Love, the capacity to love and be loved by our family, our friends, our spouses.

• Wisdom, the transcendental knowledge reserved for those few who care about something more than looking good.

• Good health, the reward of those who forget about disease and refuse to accept it or think about it.

• Joy, the feeling of inner fulfillment that comes from being satisfied and happy.

• Time, the scarce and precious resource that we must pay attention to and take full advantage of, to enjoy the above...

Money is important in each of these areas. However, our pursuit of success has to be primarily a search for balance and the equal development of mind, body and soul; not only the pursuit of money.

b. The importance of age.

Let's assume you already know what you want; but, do you have the right age for success?

Forty percent of the people do nothing with their lives because they feel they are too old to start; forty percent do nothing because they feel they are still very young; and nineteen percent do nothing because they don't know whether they are too old or too young. After years of studying the remaining 1% that do something, I've discovered the perfect age for success...

Oscar Wrigley, a UK child with an IQ of 160 —same as Albert Einstein, was admitted at two years and five months as the youngest member of Mensa (the global society of *geniuses*, people with high IQ). Kim Ung-Yong, with an IQ of 210, reached the university level at four years old, and received his doctorate at 15. Jaswal Akrit operated on his first patient at age 7, and by age 12 he was the youngest student ever admitted to a medical career at a university in India. Mozart composed his first piece when he was 5; Beethoven, when he was 11. Michael Dell, founder of Dell computers, started his company at 15. King David was a teenager when he killed Goliath.

All of this let me conclude that to succeed in life you must have done something extraordinary before you turn 18. However,

Bill Gates and Steve Jobs were 19 when they laid the foundations of Microsoft and Apple. Mark Zuckerberg founded Facebook in his early twenties. Alexander the Great became Emperor of the known world at 23. Chad Hurley, founder of YouTube, sold it to Google for $ 1.65 billion at age 29.

So, I concluded that the real age for success is between 18 and 29 years of age. However,

Jesus began preaching at 30. Jules Verne published his first novel at 35. Columbus discovered America at 46. Charles Darwin published his "Origin of the Species" at 49. Leonardo Da Vinci was 51 when he painted his masterpiece, the Mona Lisa. Nostradamus published his prophetic centuries at 52. Ray Crock, founder of the McDonald's, was a 53 year old smoothie machine salesman when he had the vision of starting his business. Abraham Lincoln was a mediocre failure until age 50, when, after the death of his beloved, had an internal transformation process that led him to become one of the most respected U.S. presidents.

Therefore, I concluded that the age for success is really between 31 and 55 years. However,

In 1931, at age 56, a man named Winston Churchill fell into a terrible depression. He had been completely isolated from politics in England, and people considered him *done*. However, he did not surrender. Nine years later, at age 65, he was appointed prime minister and led his country during World War II.

Colonel Sanders, founder of Kentucky Fried Chicken, was 65 when he started selling his chicken franchise, after a short time living of social security.

After spending 27 years in prison, Nelson Mandela, 72, led the negotiations for a multiracial democracy in South Africa, and was president from 1994-1999, leaving the term at 81 years of age. **Due to the last three cases, I concluded definitively that the age to succeed in life is between 56 and 81 years old... However,**

Today I saw in the news that Kozo Haraguchi, 95, broke the 100-meter record for people over 75...

The Truth is, there is not a right or predetermined age for success.

There are only people who finally decide to succeed.

Age is in your mind!

Never forget that we are immortal spirits, souls trapped in bodies that last, on average, about eighty years (although the number of people who pass 100 has soared thanks to medical advances). Now 50 is just t half of life. Sixties are the new forties, and forties are the new twenties (which I firmly believe, after turning forty feeling young, very very young.)

There are two types of elderly: those who long for death in an asylum at seventy, and those who await the cure to all diseases, while sailing the Mediterranean.

A few years ago, on a cruise, I made friends with an Italian couple celebrating 70 years of marriage. On our London stop, they showed us the city, walking and talking animatedly for more than four hours. My wife and I ended up seeing them as two normal friends -only wiser and full of energy-, and their age only made our trip more memorable and interesting!

With the current life expectancy, a 60 year old who wants to start a company could assume he has another twenty or even forty years to see it growing. Can you imagine what could happen in that time?

NOBODY is *finished* until his/her body is in a coffin at the cemetery. And yet ... there are those who woke up in a coffin because they were not really dead! The point is no one is too young or too old to succeed, to paint the Mona Lisa, to create a famous novel, to invent a new energy source, to discover a new atomic element, or to have an extraordinary idea.

At what age are you going to take the decision to succeed? When you do, you must then...

c. Believe in yourself

The only difference between you and the richest guy in town, or your rich uncle, or Forbes' new number 10, is not the millions, is the attitude!

In the minds of rich people -which are identical to you in everything and have the same number of cells, wealth is something over which they have no doubt.

Once you have the map and traced the route to be followed, the next step is to believe in yourself, and start walking with the full assurance that whatever happens, the universe has provided you with the irrefutable capacity to get where you want.

Believing in yourself is the only way you can achieve the goals that you dreamed about.

1. Don't preoccupy about the past. Occupy in creating the future.

You have to leave behind anything in your past that tells you that you are not an extraordinary being. No matter where it comes, what you choose to believe is what is important. Forget the past. Stop telling your friends that perhaps your life would be better or different if something had happened five or ten years ago.

It did not happen; period. You are where you are, that is reality.

However, the results from your past do not guarantee that you will get the same results in the future. You can change your future for good!

Although today's reality is the result of past behaviors, it is also true that anything you have done or have been done to you in the past -which is relevant for your present, can be changed as of now. Maybe, the change will come from the lessons learned during those difficult moments you now remember with bitterness.

But I've always failed! But I have never achieved what I set to do! But my parents didn't love me and told me bad things... If people depended on who their parents were to be successful, how come so many orphans succeed, and so many with loving parents end *stoned* in the streets?

NEVER use your present to think about our past: is the only way your future can be different from the present. As Napoleon Bonaparte said, *to hell with circumstances; I make the circumstances.* The circumstances are not important, but what is done with them.

2. The world will think of you, exactly what you think of yourself.

If you leave the house thinking you are ugly, everybody will think you are ugly. **Grandma.**

Some time ago I came across a friend who had always been considered ugly. It's cruel, but it's true. But that day she was well groomed, instead of glasses she had contacts, and was wearing, for the first time, a beautiful dress on her size. Frankly I was surprised! I had never noticed that she could actually be attractive.

Then I thought: someone convinced her many years ago that she was ugly; probably didn't even like to look in the mirror. And as my grandmother said, she would leave the house feeling ugly, and that's what everyone else saw. But the day she decided to leave the house feeling pretty, the world noticed!

How many "fools" out there are actually smart, but they don't believe it? How many talented people think they are awkward? How many good looking people think they are ugly? How many skinny people think they are fat? You... What do you think of yourself?

Are you sure you are all the bad things somebody said you were, -parents, teachers, classmates, a long lost love that left you, perhaps so long ago that you don't even remember who it was? This is one of the big problems of mankind. What others see in you is based on what you have decided to believe of yourself.

When we let someone convince us that we are little, we walk silently shouting it to all those we meet.

I will never forget Mario, my art teacher in seventh grade. He asked us to paint a shark. I took the project really seriously and invested days making sure of doing a great job! But Mario took it, gave it a quick glance, and mocked it in front of the class, convincing me for the rest of my life that I had no talent for art.

The funny thing is, my wife studied art, she has seen me drawing sometimes -when I strip of my complex, and is convinced that in fact I'm good! What would have happened if such an unintelligent teacher had told me, instead, that I had done well, but maybe I just had to try harder? I'm not saying I would have been the next Picasso, but why not? However, since I didn't believe in myself, and let Mario convince me of my lack of talent, I developed a phobia of art and I never, never, ever, painted anything.

And don't get me talking about football! I never played as a kid; somebody convinced me I was 'bad'. I started playing at 35! Now I play every week, I love it, and I even score a pair of goals hear and then!

How hard it was to overcome my insecurities and to believe in myself, even when I was financially "*successful*"!

The first one that has to believe in you is YOURSELF. If not, you could convince even your own mother that you are not capable of greatness

3. Your environment is fundamental.

Surround yourself with snakes, and they will poison you.

Surround yourself with eagles, and you will learn to fly to the heavens.

The fact that we are always learning and changing from positive or negative influences is another powerful reason why your environment is critical to success.

It is such basic knowledge; but it is incredible how much people need to hear it again and again:

Surround yourself with successful and positive people who say good things and support you. And stay away from negative people, those who criticize you, call you crazy and tell you that whatever you want "is impossible

Whenever somebody who did achieve something amazing is interviewed, the first thing he or she says is "I'm glad I did not listen to the people who told me that I couldn't do it."

Try to imagine for a moment all the great things, the talented people, the fabulous works, the revolutionary inventions ... that we have lost because some LISTENED to the negative people around them.

What a terrible tragedy!

Do not worry about what other people say about your dreams. Never seek *advice* except from those who will tell you *"yes, you can"*. There is a reason why the creative energy gave that dream or talent to you and not to the person in front of you who is now telling you *it is impossible*.

Trust your inner voice.

When others tell you what they think of "your reality" or your dreams, they are projecting what they think of themselves and their ability to achieve their own dreams. It has nothing to do with you. You are not them. People have problems believing what they don't understand. They think their limitations are the pattern for everybody else's limitations!

Steve Jobs was called by Apple's board *'an irresponsible dreamer'*. He was betrayed and sacked from his own company... But he did not stop and cry. He simply analyzed the situation, learned the lessons, recharged forces, and dedicated his energy to create Pixar, which he later sold to Disney. Years later, he returned to rescue Apple from its imminent bankruptcy, and led them in revolutionizing the world with their products.

Imagine if he would have just sat down and thought of himself as a failure!

Don't ever let anyone belittle you.

Do you know the names of those who fired Jobs for being a 'dreamer'? NO! The story does not remember negative fools, or if does, is just to mock them.

Great people have built their lives and success with the stones others have thrown at them. They did not focus on the wounds or the pain; or cried thinking about their flaws or mistakes or what others *thought* of them. They focused on their strengths and talents.

Do the same!

Don't forget that you are a special being created for a great mission... You have within the seeds of success, wisdom and prosperity. You are worth more than you think and what you credit yourself for...

Focus on your successes!

4. Make your mind a castle. Change your expectations!

Success is not a privilege of the smart, the beautiful or those who have the money; or of all your friends except you. It is a privilege of those who accept that they are full of potential and believe that are capable of achieving it.

People fill their minds with negative thoughts they repeat to their subconscious. And then, when as a result something negative happens, they convince themselves it is all they deserve.

Both the most beautiful castle and the more horrid prison, have a floor, concrete walls and a roof... The materials are the same. It is what the builder does with the material that makes all the difference.

Change the walls of your mind -walls full of obstacles and negative images about yourself, with walls of achievement, confidence and faith.

You are the builder of your life. Build a Castle!

Free will means that you can order the materials you want. If you want dirt floors, cold walls and ceilings painted with graffiti, you will get that. If you want marble floors, beautiful colored walls, and ceilings decorated with unique frescoes, ask that, and that is what you will get.

Ask and you shall receive.

Ask... and you shall receive!

Rich people attract wealth because they believe it is *the normal thing* and they *deserve it*. So, that is what they ask and receive.

> *Before having what you want, you have to believe that you can get it.*
>
> *Only then you could see it happening.*

Stop limiting yourself to "little things", and believe that you deserve success and prosperity. Run away from the mentality of poverty, from "I don't deserve it, that's not for me".

If you use the words "I can't do it", "I can't buy it", "I can't, I can't, I can't", your subconscious will obey literally, and not only won't help you overcome obstacles, but will prevent you from doing it. Why? Because your subconscious actually believes that is pleasing you, fulfilling your wishes, doing what you asked. After all, you always say you can't...

On this subject, I recommend the book "The Power of the Subconscious Mind" by Joseph Murphy. After reading it you will be totally convinced that anything you *program* in your subconscious, whether positive or negative, HAPPENS.

Ask and you shall receive.

Ask... and you shall receive!

My daughter always says that the saying "*seeing is believing*" is the opposite of faith. Having faith means you first have to believe in order to see. How can you get things that you can't even dream? So, believe!

Belief controls our path to success. Keep your expectations high; develop the mentality of "believing it" as the Chinese did. When I see what is happening in China or India, countries that were poor 20 years ago and today are rich, I see people like you or me who changed their EXPECTATIONS. They focused on creating, they believed, and they were successful! The parable was clear: only to those who earn more, shall more be given.

But remember that the mindset has to be creation and not competition. This means that you should not want or envy what another has. Create your own dreams, your own things. Never envy the neighbor's house, if you want a house like your neighbor's, build it, create it... Or remember there are millions of beautiful empty houses waiting for you!

And never forget to apply, always and at every moment, the principle of gratitude. We all love to be thanked when we do something good or give something to someone. Who says The Creator of the Universe is different? Start thanking and be grateful for all that you have and all that you are getting. You will see how, almost magically, you get more...

d. Do not be afraid of failure

If you go to my website, you can buy for only $19.95 (free shipping), a powerful talisman submerged in oil of an Amazon tree, discovered during my last trip. With it you will never be touched by failure...

Ha! I bet more than one went running to buy the talisman. I have news. The Talisman ... does not exist! And the Amazon tree... maybe... No!!! In fact, I've never been to the Amazon, although I want to go.

Failure is not something that comes out of nowhere, because someone voodoos us with an evil eye.

Another step towards success is to understand that failure is the accumulation of small errors that add up. It is like a glass that gradually fills, drop by drop, until the cup overflows. It does not appear by magic; it does not mean God is punishing us. No! Like everything in life -such as growth, such as achieving our goals, failure is a process.

Now, don't get depressed if you have failed. Although we have to try and keep failure as far as possible, we can use it as a tool for success.

In fact, the most successful people made many mistakes; but they learned their lessons, stood up, and kept trying to fulfill their dreams −unlike those left behind. Napoleon Hill, who wrote *Think and Grow Rich* after interviewing the 500 richest men of his time, concluded that most of them found their greatest achievements after their biggest failures.

In every failure, there's the seed to even greater success. However, people waste their time complaining, instead of looking for the seed among the rubble of what was.

Many authors use the example of Thomas Edison's 10,000 attempts to create the light bulb. What would have happened if he would have said *I've tried 2000 times and nothing. This must be God telling me not to do it; it is a sign... My enemies probably casted an evil spell on me...* The world would probably be darker at night! (Or we would be using Tesla technology, but, that's for another book!)

Did you know that the discovery of America and the construction of the Tower of Pisa were two of the most famous failures in history? Columbus failed to reach Asia, as was his dream. But the end result was far greater. And Bonnano Pisano made in 1173 the mistake of building a tower in a place without good foundations (such was the fiasco that the work was abandoned to its fate!) He could have never suspected that his "failure" would make his city famous in the world, and that the Tower of Pisa would be the economic engine of its region through tourism.

Life is like a video game. We move forward when we learn the tricks of each level. How do we learn the tricks? Most need to experience on their own, because that's how we learned to learn...

If you have experienced a failure, take time to analyze, write, meditate and study the mistakes. This way you can turn it into stepping stones to opportunity. If you learn the lessons, you would never make the same mistake again, and change your destiny. And above all, don't give up, keep trying, and...

e. Prepare constantly

Success is a plant that needs to be watered every day. Without water; if you fail to tend to it, it dies.

And on that waterless soil, from the withered stalks of abandoned success, almost imperceptibly, the weed of failure is born...

Although it sounds cliché, that's a good metaphor.

Therefore, PREPARE YOURSELF!

Read and listen to as many audiobooks and CD's on success and self-improvement as you can get. Ask your friends to give you material; borrow it from public libraries. Expend a few dollars and buy some books (especially, if they are written by me... See, another ad.) But commit yourself to a constant search for good ideas and motivational phrases.

Sometimes a phrase we read or hear just clicks and suddenly our body triggers. I remember a particular moment when I listened to the words of the creator of Nike, which I mentioned in the preface. *"People will remember only our last victory and not our past failures."* I heard it at a time I was feeling so defeated! But more than that, I felt embarrassed with the world, since I could not find -and I knew no one could find a justification for my situation.

Being told, even in if was by a CD, that one day people would not think about my failures, but only about my last victory, made me get up from the chair and get to work. But I heard that phrase, because I was looking for motivation; because I had sought information and I had read several books. Sooner or later, the phrase had to come and it did!

I ask you: What do you need to be told to stop thinking about your problems, and start calling success? So you will begin to believe with all your heart that you can do it? What is your magic phrase?

Watching the news and listening to rap will hardly do it. Well, there's a song that says "I like to move it, move it" Ha! I must confess that the advice "do what you love", is a great tip. I really enjoy myself when I write. But that's a side note.

Now what authors cannot be missed in your collection? No doubt, those of great teachers like Orison Swett Marden (more than 50 amazing books); Napoleon Hill "Think and Grow Rich", Wallace Wattles, with "The Science of Getting Rich" and his other books, and William Walker Atkinson with over 100 books (all these books are part of the Timeless Wisdom Collection, to which this book belongs).

90% of books on success are founded on the principles of these authors. Some are nothing but copies. Other, updated examples disguised as originality. But if you want to go to the source, this is it; and they are available everywhere in the Internet, mostly for free.

Another great author is Jim Rohn, mentor to many other very famous authors. Listen to anything of him and you will feel compelled to take action. I also like Bryan Tracy, Zig Ziglar, Tony Robbins, and Bob Proctor and T. Harv Ecker. But if you've never read anything, start with Marden, Hill, Walker and Wattles, then Jim Rohn, and the others in the order I suggest.

Believe me, you will never, never, never regret it, and your life will change for the better. That's a universal truth, but only if what you hear or read does not go in one ear and out the other.

As I said, it is important to water the plant, and do it consistently. They say the fuel of a good motivational book lasts very active the first week ... then begins to dissipate, and in a month, we barely remember.

Some time ago I was invited to a meeting of a multi-level marketing company. Although I attended out of courtesy, I must acknowledge that I left completely surprised (and almost sold!) I was admired to see how constantly they motivate each other. For three hours we heard about the successes of others, testimonies of achievement, and 'yes, you can!'

Awards were given for goals achieved; for obstacles overcame; to the best seller of the week, the month, the year... Whoever wasn't motivated out there desperately needs a transplant of emotions!

All multilevel marketing schemes are based on constant motivation and in permanently thinking about success. They have people read and listen everything they can to stay "tuned". Whoever designed those systems clearly understood that human beings work by motivation, and they did it extremely well.

You are a human being. Motivate and cheer yourself! Give yourself rewards every time you reach a goal! Only good things will come out of it.

Now, continuing with the sources of wisdom and motivation, I can't leave out the most special one. During my "*sabbatical*" year, I had the opportunity to do what I recommend here: study, read a lot and listen to every single audio book I could get. For me, it was a crash course; a rare opportunity life gave me.

And if something I understood was that if in the middle of my business career, during my wandering from here to there, I would had taken the time to study not just the latest marketing tool, or the latest best seller on planning and budget, but simple and basic principles of wisdom, many errors would had not been committed.

Do you know one of the secrets of the most powerful people in the world? Finally revealed after thousands of years... If you keep reading maybe I tell you...

See? You kept reading! The secret is the Wisdom of Solomon and other sages. The most successful people usually confess in their biographies about reading- and applying, The Proverbs. No wonder Solomon is considered the richest man who ever lived, much more than Gates, Slim or Buffet, *combined*.

And if I would have done a quarter of what Solomon says my story would have been so different!

Do not reject this source only *because "it is in the Bible and probably talks about religion."* Or because *"I'm agnostic."* Whatever works for you. However, consider this source! And when you do, you will realize that most business Best Sellers rely on it for advice and the most popular sayings come from there.

Proverbs has 31 chapters, with 20-30 sentences each. If you read a chapter a day, in a month you would finish it. From chapter 10 on, it consists of very simple sentences, full of wise advice. If you read a little every day, for a year, you will register the knowledge and hopefully, it is going to make you wiser. Or at least you will always have a "clever phrase" to respond to others.

On believing everything people tell you, Proverbs 14:15 says: "The naive believe everything, but the shrewd watch their steps." Proverbs 22: 3. "A prudent man sees danger and hides while the naive continue on and pay the price."

About being a guarantor of your debts friends, Proverbs 22:26-27 says: "Do not be one of those who give their hand in pledge, those who become surety for debts; for if you are unable to pay, your bed will be taken from under you."

Other sources similar to Proverbs, are Ecclesiastes and Sirach (only in Catholic Bibles) Sirach 6, 12 and 13 talks about "friends" and partners. Although written 2200 years ago, describes at least 50% of the people you know. Or 95%? Judge it yourself. Read it, it will be good as part of your business success and education, and will possibly help you to see who your friends really are. Just leave you with this one: Sirach 12: 8-9 "In prosperity we cannot know our friends; in adversity an enemy will not remain concealed. When one is successful even an enemy is friendly; but in adversity even a friend disappears."

f. Be generous!

The final principle of this short introduction to success is associated with a tricky and almost scary subject. An especially painful one... It is easier to convince people that bats are just hamsters with cute wings, than of the fact that taking money out their pocket for something that does not gratify or benefit them immediately and directly, can be good somehow.

However, the principle of giving is universal to all religions and philosophies throughout history.

Bill Gates and Warren Buffet, the richest men in the world, decided to donate 50% of their fortunes to charity (about 50 billion U.S. dollars). Not only that; they are promoting dinner meetings throughout the United States with groups of multimillionaires, to convince them that the best they can do with their money is to donate it to foundations! The funny thing is that these two are perhaps the only ones in the world who can convince a lot of people that getting rid of their money is not only correct, but deeply cool. 50 billionaires have already agreed to donate half of their fortunes!

Now, you don't need to be billionaire or millionaire. If you use part of your income to help others when their situation is not their best, for some reason, everything starts to work out.

However, there are a couple of rules to remember:

First, do it because it is right. Give with love, or how do I say it to sound *politically correct?* Give because you feel it's good to do so; because you feel it inside of you; because you see others in need -children that need food, old people in need of shelter, and you feel it is your human duty to help because you understand you are part of the same energy that is in everything and everyone else.

Don't do it because somebody pressured or manipulated you, or because *"God will give you back a hundredfold"*. If you give because it is right and proper, you will comply with the command to '*seek first the kingdom of God and his righteousness, and all these things will be added to you.'* And the additions may mean the multiplication of your money. But if you give just because you expect your money back multiplied, you are not fulfilling your duty to help others or doing it for the right reasons.

Secondly, don't do it to be "seen". Something happened to me once. I donate some money, and because it was a high profile case, I was on TV, smiling, full of myself... Then, for the first time in my life things started to go wrong. I gave the money for the right reasons, I think, but I must confess that I liked my fifteen seconds of fame... And since not only my left hand, but the whole country, learned of what I had done, the blessing didn't work, and it rather became a problem.

So, set aside part of your income to do good deeds, to help nursing homes, to support your church, orphanages, or to give a scholarship to a smart child who may not have the resources and you will never lack anything. And remember, *giving* is not only about material things. Sometimes the most valuable thing you can give someone is time, support, guidance, good advice.

Be a mentor, be a friend, teach others the principles for success you learned in this book.

As my grandmother would say, *"hands that give are never empty."*

PART TWO.
Laying The Foundations
Of Your Business.

Now that you have the mental tools to believe in yourself, to dream, and to take action, you must learn how to make your businesses become successful, by building solid foundations.

A business is like a house: you have to take extraordinary care in laying strong foundations. If this principle is violated, subsidence and cracks will follow, and though the walls may look solid, sooner or later the house may fall or has to be demolished.

LAW #3
PAY ATTENTION TO NUMBERS AND FINANCES.

Money management is key in any business; therefore the first advice for entrepreneurs is in this area. You could be brilliant, have the greatest idea or product in the world, the best of intentions, but if you are not wise at managing your finances, at the end of the day everything else will matter very little.

a. Be careful doing your numbers!

If you made it this far, you probably really want to be an entrepreneur and make money with your effort. It is in something you like. You are willing to make sacrifices and to lay good foundations for your company. You are ready to go!

What is the first thing you do to determine if an idea works as a business? **You *"crunch"* the numbers.** And one of the biggest mistakes entrepreneurs -large or small make, is the tendency to be extremely optimistic and to do what my Dad always refers as *"crunching happy numbers."*

Happy numbers are over optimistic profit estimates which are not based on a realistic or comprehensive cost analysis.

Ultimately, the success or failure of a company depends on how well these *numbers* are *crunched*.

Let me illustrate this concept with a simple example that contains a lot of truths.

Let's imagine we want to sell hot dogs. If we are like any other human being —and many, many corporations, the first calculation we tend to make is: *"If I sell a thousand hot dogs for $10 each, I MAKE TEN THOUSAND DOLLARS!"*

Then, after the initial euphoria, we do a deeper *analysis,* and realize we must subtract the cost of the bun and of the sausage. Let's say it is $5 per hot dog. This means *we still make five thousand!* And that's only in the first 1000 doggies! Done deal! Decided! We are going to sell hot dogs, right? ¡NOOOO! ¡ALTO!

NOO! STOP! That's NOT how things work.

Remember that I mentioned in the introduction that 50% of business shut up shop in the first year? I also told you that another 40% close within 3 years. The sad thing is that within the 40% that keep trying for a while, there are huge numbers that "break even" or lose money, having to come with money from other businesses or jobs for something that is failing, until they finally accept it and close.

And they fail because they forget to consider the *other costs...* Ketchup, chopped onions, tomatoes, napkins or the paper boxes for the hot dog. Worse yet, they forget rent, utilities, and the employee's salary (which will also give away dogs to his friends, and eat a few, as we will discuss later.)

Since they forget all that, they never realize that each hot dog really cost $9. So, after working, coordinating, running and making a great effort, the final "profit" was not even $1 per dog! Or even worse, they never discover on time that the hot dogs cost more than the $10 they charged, so besides work, they had to come with money off their pocket!

Yes, it's that hard. Not always, but it's that hard. And if you think I'm exaggerating, ask your entrepreneur friends. We all have come across things like that. It is part of what we call *getting business experience.*

I know so many intelligent people which made this mistake and are traumatized for life. They had the talent, ideas and the wish to make the necessary sacrifices to undertake extraordinary endeavors and become entrepreneurs; but failed because of poor planning.

b. Find all your costs!

So, if you don't want this to happen to you or to acquire experience the hard way, you should always plan for the *worst case scenario.*

Before starting anything, sit down and consider **absolutely all** costs in a completely honest and realistic way. From gas to go to the supermarket to buy bread and sausages; to the buns that fell apart or the sausages that went bad because you forgot to put them in the fridge (or *"contingencies"*). Find those hidden expenses that seem to bury in secret nooks. Everything means everything. We may fool others but not ourselves: we are the ones that feel it in our wallets.

If your business survives to this analysis, then it is viable. The opposite takes us to another truth:

There are bad businesses; ideas that are not profitable. It is up to you to find out before you start; or to wait until you have lost everything!

So, let's say you just realized the dogs cost $10 and, since you were going to sell them for $10, there was no profit. How sad, no? No! Be happy! You just avoid going through the process most entrepreneurs go: they realize it after, not before.

Now, don't get discouraged! Most businesses have the potential to make profits. Sometimes you only need to be more careful with costs. If costs are tight, but you still believe it can be good business, sit down, twitch things a little and look for ways to make things work. THERE ARE SOLUTIONS; IT IS ONLY A MATTER OF LOOKING FOR THEM.

What I am suggesting is to be careful and thorough to avoid the trap of *happy numbers*. In other words, go about your business with an *optimistic realism*.

It's sad to work and work and work and work, to find out at the end of the month that -how strange, there is nothing left but debts! If you have ever experienced this, the most likely cause is that you don't know your true costs, that you have not sat down to crunch numbers, because the words planning or budget sound ugly and you imagine huge Excel sheets with projections that not even your accountant understands.

You would be surprised of how many people haven't realized they are selling for a loss. They are *a sensation* in sales, killing the competition... But they are selling so cheap they are losing money!

Don't join that group. It's not fair to you, and eventually the ones who win -those who buy, in most cases will not be grateful. And if you sell on credit, the chances are high they don't even pay!

Obviously this example is an oversimplification of an immensely complex issue. Unfortunately, it happens to the car dealer, the builder, and the owner of the store at the Mall.

The truth is, some entrepreneurs end up living of the credit card, because they refuse to admit their numbers don't add up and their business can't pay the bills. Credit cards have contributed to us deluding ourselves, so we don't make adjustments in time until we are terribly in debt.

I am not suggesting you to be negative. No. Optimism; Positive Thinking; to believe in ourselves, it's all necessary and good! If we wouldn't believe in ourselves, we would all be employees of large corporations! And there is always the need for entrepreneurs, the strength and blood of any economy.

So, sit down, do realistic calculations, find out solutions and do the necessary

1. *Do you need or can afford employees?* If so, get good ones who doesn't steal or eat the *hot dogs*. Or maybe you sell very little Monday through Friday -say, 75 dogs in five days, but sell 200 on weekends. Therefore, you should attend the business yourself rather than having employees, and continue in your regular job while the business grows and matures.

2. *Could you reduce contingencies?* For example, if you know which products are easily damaged in the warehouse or in transit, why don't you ask everyone to be more careful? Recently, a glass containers manufacturer had to cut wages because of the recession. For 50 years the historic waste contingency (for broken bottles and others) was 15%. The owner offered employees that if they cut waste, 100% of the savings would go to supplement their wages. THEY REDUCED WASTE BY HALF! In other words, the money and the potential savings were always there.

3. *Could you get better prices for your supplies?* Maybe you are using expensive sausages instead of ones that taste good and cost half (don't overdo it; don't kill quality). Perhaps you're buying bread in packages of 6 instead of 100; or using brand name ketchup instead of generic from Wal-Mart; or buying onions and tomatoes at the supermarket instead of the farmer's market.

However, it is not about saving for the sake of saving! Sometimes, trying to save a dime on a key thing ends up costing thousands of dollars. We once built 10 homes, and installed a plastic piece in the concrete slab under the bath tubs. The expensive piece cost $7, but we used a generic one that looked the same and cost $2, for a total savings of $50. The piece failed, we had to break the slab, and the repair cost over $2,000 per house, a total of $ 20,000!

It is about finding the best suppliers, not only price-wise but in quality and reliability. There is nothing worse than a supplier who doesn't deliver on time and forces us to stop production; or who sells us a defective part and we end up losing money and reputation!

4. *Is your price right?* Perhaps all you need is a slight price increase. Say you decide to sell the dogs at $12 instead of $10. Let me tell you something: 90% of your customers won't even notice. And you will finally receive something for your effort!

It is all about common sense. The goal is to avoid being one of those that sells thousands of units before realizing they had done wrong numbers or calculations, and lost it all...

c. Reinvest

Let's assume you did all the right calculations; the business has potential; you sold a thousand hot dogs and received ten or twelve thousand dollars...

You have no idea how many *entrepreneurs* take that money, and SPEND IT ALL! And forget to buy more bread and sausages to sell more hot dogs!

Most people want to start a business today, and within a month, have money to buy a big TV, put a down payment on a car, and move to a bigger house! We are *entrepreneurs* now; we *must* live better, right? Some would buy the TV and forget to put money aside for the newspaper ad that would generate new customers; or neglect to buy the machine that would increase production. Or use the employees' wages to make the car down payment; or end up buying lower quality inputs because they ran out of money!

If you are determined to be a serious entrepreneur and make things work, you can not violate the principle of reinvesting in your business. I'm going to say something that no entrepreneur wants to hear:

You are not entitled to spend the company's money until it is mature, well established, the foundations are laid on firm soil, and is producing real profits.

If the farmer gets hungry and eats the seed, how will he have a harvest? **Don't eat the seed.** The revenues of your business are seeds, not petty cash. If you need to live of your company, pay yourself a salary it can afford. Work for that salary and live within your means. Even if you are the owner, your business needs the seed for future harvest.

d. Beware of debt-based growth.

It hurts me just to think about this.

I used to boast that by applying this principle I had created a multimillion dollar company! It works like this. I have $50, and I get an *opportunity* that requires an investment of $100. So I invest my $50 and borrow $50. I do well, and my $50 becomes $200. Now, a $400 opportunity arises. I invest my $200, and borrow $200. I do well and finish with $800. Wow! I am a genius! Now I am ready for the big leagues: the $1600 opportunity. I have $800, I borrow $800, take the risk...

In this *gambler's scenario,* we lose sight of the fact that the risk is getting bigger and if something goes wrong, it's harder to pay interest or principal on a biggest debt. Secondly, if we are like most people, the $800 we invested is ALL we have –an all or nothing scenario, and we have no reserves. In other words, we throw ourselves without a parachute, hoping, as usual, to land in our feet. The problem with tempting destiny is that, one of those times, we may not land that well. Even worst, we may land head on, and kill ourselves!

e. Cash is King.

This famous phrase should be a little different: "No cash is dumb!" It is hard to believe there are companies worth millions of dollars with no cash in the bank, always depending on a miracle! But there are more of those than you may think...

Every company should have a cash fund; a *skinny cows cushion*, with a size directly proportional to the size of the company. A small business facing cash flow problems can be saved by an uncle or a cousin who miraculously appeared and gave a loan. However, some companies become so large that the only uncle who can save them is Uncle Sam ... and sometimes not even The President can save you! When you live in the razor's edge, sooner or later, you get cut...

> ***Cash is king.*** *No matter how many good opportunities come your way, do not invest all your cash. If you run out of reserves, the smallest or foolish of things may bring you down. Companies with millions in assets have gone bankrupt because they cannot make a $25,000 payment. It's hard, but it's true.*

f. Do not commingle funds

This is a very difficult problem; to avoid it requires a lot of discipline to fight temptation. If you have more than one company, and you constantly mix their funds, you can de-capitalize a self-sufficient company, to fund a *dead body,* a company you should have buried long ago, closed it and forgotten it, but you are taking money from successful companies to buy expensive perfumes to keep the *dead one* smelling good.

In 2010 I buried my last dead *body,* a company that never made any money. I kept it because of pride -I was afraid of the "public" embarrassment; and I was deceiving myself into believing that someday it would be successful. I lost millions over ten years. How hard I worked in other companies to keep that one "alive"!

Don't make that mistake! Don't take money from a successful business, to try to save a failing one. You will end up losing both

When Steve Jobs bought Pixar, he gave it capital, the necessary tools, and said 'there is no more money; the company has to stay afloat by itself'. And Pixar succeeded. When companies know they have to survive on their own, somehow they do. When they know there are deep pockets ready to bail them out of problems, almost inevitably they fall on them.

g. Save!

Prov.21-20 "A fool spends all that he has" *Prov.21-20*

Prov.16-20 "Whoever is doing well managed well"

"Did you eat ***all*** the ice **cream?"** *My mom.*

Do you remember when as a child, your parents taught you about saving? It was always about skipping candy and putting the money in the piggy bank instead. At the end of the year, those *un-eaten* chocolates or candies could be transformed into some fashionable sneakers or jeans to impress your friends.

Of course, when having to decide between eating the candy or saving, we were invaded by an irresistible desire for the sweets. However, if good habits prevailed and we saved, the prize at the end was always pleasant, and we in turn avoided cavities or being obese.

I'll tell you a secret: *I was a fat kid!* I think my problems as an entrepreneur started because I always ate all the candy. I ate all the chocolates and all the ice cream I could find. I loved it! And I never had the discipline to save in the piggy bank (and therefore, did not have any money to buy my gift at the end of the year). *I ATE IT ALL!*

My brother Gilberto, a year younger than I, received the same amount of money. However, he was the other extreme. When he felt hungry at school, he drank water until he was filled, and he saved everything in the Bank! He had one of those children savings accounts; and at age 16 he had enough money to buy equipment and start his own business.

Me, on the other hand, had just entered college, and was glad that -after paying a gym for a full year- I was finally thin!

*Saving entails sacrifice; and maybe that's why it brings rewards. **Those that save always have.** If tomorrow you face a problem -you lose your job or your business, you know you can survive until the situation improves or you start another business, this time with firm foundations. However those that do not save... Do you need me to tell you?*

Great writers on this subject -as Bryan Tracy and George Clason (in *The Richest Man in Babylon*), say you should save 10% of all income. What does it means for you? Not going to nice restaurants this month? Driving a Toyota instead of a Lexus? Living in a house with three bedrooms and not four?

If you can get in the habit of saving 10% (they say it must be the first thing you take from your check, just close your eyes, put it in the Bank and forget it exists), it is possible that you don't get used to the opposite: to spend more than you earn, and cover the difference with credit cards and high interest loans, making you a slave for life.

PRINCIPLES OF THE CHAPTER

• We tend to crunch HAPPY NUMBERS, not considering all the actual costs involved in the product or service we sell. However, always remember: if you don't set out clearly and honestly all your costs, you are doomed to lose money and to get loans to cover the consequences of your lack of planning.

• Before selling your product, find absolutely all costs involved. Don't leave out anything. If you don't know how much it costs, how on earth would you set the price?

• It takes not only bread and sausages; but Ketchup, mustard, chopped onion, napkins; rent; wages of employees; utilities; and indirect costs such as gasoline to go and buy the bread.

• If the price is not competitive, you can see what adjustments can be done. Change suppliers, slightly reduce portions. Think!

Reinvest in your business. You are not entitled to use it for petty cash to buy a new house or travel the world ... before it is firmly established, and producing real profits. That will come in time, be patient. If you eat the seeds, how will you reap some day?

• Cash is king. Never use all your cash pursuing new opportunities. If you run out of cash, you may lose what you have.

• **Do not** grow too much based on debt. If something goes wrong, a small amount of interest can bring down a multimillion dollar company.

• **Do not** commingle funds between companies. You can de-capitalize a successful one to finance a loser that you should have closed a long time ago. The dead is dead. Accept it, cry it, bury it and forget it.

• If a business is not profitable, just get another one! Keep thinking. One idea that failed is not the end of the world. Above all, do not be the stubborn who ignored his own instincts (or who simply didn't plan) and end up losing everything.

• Save 10 % of what you make. If it means skipping a couple of fancy restaurants, that is preferable to someday having to ask a loan to be able to eat. You don't have to drive the best car or live in the biggest house either. Two of the world's richest men, Warren Buffett and Walmart's Sam Walton (whose heirs are 5 to 8 among the richest in the world) always lived in the same house, without ostentation, and drove the same old car for many years. That is a little too much... However, you get the idea.

• Bryan Tracy says that Money likes to be respected. When you save, you will not only be better prepared to sort out bad times, but will attract more money. Somehow having something in the bank attracts more money and opportunities. And peace... There is nothing more relaxing than knowing that even if things go wrong, we will be okay...

LAW #4.
KEEP FOCUSED; GROW WISELY; CHOOSE YOUR OPPORTUNITIES

There is no greater fortune and joy than to have a fulfilling job or to own a business that we love.

I do what I like and I make money of it?

When we do what we love and use the hours in our true passion, energy seems endless. It's like a car. Going uphill, up and up, it uses more gas; but on a flat highway at 80 MPH, gasoline will last and last...

Since it does not feel like a great effort, and if on top we are doing well financially (which is usually the result of being focused), we begin to feel that we have time and energy for more...

However, this extra energy can make us fall into the temptation of ambition, leading us to the great curse of losing focus. Never forget a day has only twenty-four hours, and you only have a limited amount of strength.

a. If you own a store, *be there*, or you will have it no more.

> *It is the man who has his purpose burned into every fiber of his being, who has the faculty of focusing his scattered energies on one point as a burning glass focuses the scattered rays of the sun, who succeeds. Orison Swett Marden in "Prosperity, How to Attract It."*

I mentioned my brother and his good habits for saving. Well, he is also one of the most successful entrepreneurs I know. He is organized, hardworking and above all, tremendously focused. People come to him with all kinds of *good deals* (even me!). But he had remained true to his principles and to the company he started at age 16, which has grown into the largest in Central America in its field.

He has never accepted to get into businesses that are not part of what he does and is the best at doing. And surely if he ever violates this principle he would be making a huge mistake.

By staying focused -devoting all his energy to his company, and *being always there*, he is making sure he will keep being the best and remain in the market for many years.

Here I go back to Mr. Jewish Entrepreneur dad (the same that taught the lesson to his child!). He always said: ***My son, if you own a store, be there, or you will have it no more. TAKE CARE OF IT! And do it with all your might.***

Whenever I explain this point, I give a very real and scary example. Let's say you are a successful entrepreneur. You made your numbers and projections correctly, and know that if you work hard, your company is going to make a profit of $100.000 this year.

48

However, because you are doing so well, everyone wants to do business with you, right?

One day, you bump into a friend from school you have not seen in a long time. It turns out that he has a very good idea! He has been looking for someone like you. What's more, definitely, life brought you together. It's destiny; say no more. You are the perfect partner for that business. And it is so easy; it is like money in your pocket!

The idea is a Teak Wood plantation almost ready to harvest. You know nothing about it -you don't even recycle, but your friend is a forestry engineer, and he knows! You analyze the numbers, it sounds good (it was destiny, right?), and you realize that if all goes well, you could make an extra 60K from this deal.

And the truth is you have some extra time. Your current business is going smoothly, and you really don't have to be in your business all the time, because you have good assistants to handle things. Besides, you have read in books you have to learn to delegate.

So -you conclude-, with the same time and similar effort, this year you can make 160K instead of 100K.

Sounds familiar? If you are a businessperson, and by definition, someone who likes business, I know this has happened to you.

.Now, instead of one, you have two businesses.

'I am an entrepreneur with several companies. This is the start of my empire... What a success!'

While in your *tycoon* mood, you go to another party, and the same happens. Another friend, another business idea (this time, something about growing butterflies, which, believe it or not, is a real business!), you do the numbers...

With three businesses, I will make 200K this year! Twice what I thought I was going to make! Thank God for this opportunity!

You pray and give thanks, because now you are about to hit a home run and get into the major leagues, right? **WRONG! WRONG! WRONG!**

Do you remember about the day having only 24 hours? And about you having a limited amount of energy? And about the secret to success being Focused?

So, let's see what is going to happen to you.

Now you have to supervise three businesses, two of which you don't even like. And most likely you have to run from one place to the other all day, having to *'change mental tapes'*.

Marketing meeting for the Butterfly business at one. One thirty meeting with a new customer for the clothing business (Gosh, I am getting late, because I'm stuck in this butterflies meeting! I'll be there at two. Well, he is a small client. Not that important. .At two thirty I have to call the Attorney who is drafting that contract. Well, I'll read it on a hurry. The attorney knows anyway... And I asked him to keep it simple. At three reforestation meeting; there is an ant attack? That's weird. I have never heard of that. Well, I don't know anything about trees; I used to skip my biology class. What else... Oh, yes! I have to set some time to file the theft report on the factory. And what will I do with that guy? I need to fire him, I know he is stealingi But I have no time today... Okay, I'll write it down and do it tomorrow...Oops, tomorrow! I have to go on a field trip out of town! Gosh! I told the Bank I would send the new proposal to refinance the farm tomorrow. Oopsss The proposal!!!! I completely forgot about that! I have to write it. I need an all-nighter. But I can't! Tonight is my son's presentation at school. Well, he will understand if I can't make it, I'm doing this for them... And the copies... I didn't make the copies... What? The internet is down? Yes, it was due and I forgot to pay it! ¡AHHHHHHHHHH! And... And... And.... AHHHHHH!

Are you stressed out? I am, even if I wrote it... It reminded me of my life a few years ago ... Inhale ... Exhale ... Inhale ... Exhale...

Do you remember that, at the beginning of the year, you knew your company was going to make you a 100K, and you were happy? It was not a lot, but it was enough.

And before going into so many things, you were able to play golf on Tuesdays and Tennis on Thursdays. And your wife was happy because you had no belly, you got home early, you take her to dinner all the time and paid attention to your son... Or your husband was happy because you had the time to go to the gym, talk to your friends, and you did not ask him all the time if you looked fat!

Then, what in the world happened? *You let ambition complicate your life!*

If you are reading this and feel identified, do not stress out. Relax... We are all the same and this has happened to everybody. It is not the end of the world.

We all were convinced that life was about making money and more money, and then a little more.

However, even if you feel like Superman, you have the capacity to handle WELL only a limited number of things. Especially if you are a small business person, and you don't have a good team behind you (it takes years to form!). Women sometimes can handle several things at once. But men can't. If you are a man, answer me this: Have you ever tried to watch television and pay attention to your wife, both at once?

Let me tell you what happened to the businesses.

The butterflies died because of a virus (actually, they were stolen, but since you didn't have time to check, you believed the virus story!). And since your *partner* never invested any money... Instead of making 60K you ended up losing 15K.

The Teak Wood plantation... A plague of ants attacked and destroyed it! Do you think it is a joke? It did happen to me in the year 2000. I didn't know that leaf-cutting ants could eat a whole teak plantation...

However ... you know what? Now that I think about it, I do remember sending lots of money to 'combat' the scourge, but I never saw the ants! I didn't have the time to go and visit the property. Gosh... I think I get it now... 10 years later I finally got it! Ants? Yeah, right! Okay, moving on before I develop an ulcer. When my wife reads this, she is going to kill me!

Okay. Let's say that you sold the teak property, recovered the investment and *'made'* 5K. Not even for gas... but not bad, considering...

Finally, on your original business, the one good from the start, the one that was going to give you 100K... For as you were not there to control and make decisions (*you were not taking care of your store!*), thank God that you made 75K.

The only problem was that poor Mary, your assistant, ended up so fused that she resigned and decided to start her own baking cakes business!

So, you went from 100K almost sure at the beginning of the year to 60K ... all because ambition got the best of you. And you ended up working three times as much and suffered three times as much... Sad, but true.

If you focus all your energy in the right spot, there will always be good results.

However, if you disperse it in all directions, it will be so weak that it can't make an impact.

Don't get involved in so many things. It is not worth it. Go slowly; little by little. Breathe... I know, I know. The others reading the book also know.

Relax... If this example hits home, and you are still in the middle of the mess, start taking steps to get out of it. You will go crazy and will not maximize profits. But if this had never happened to you... close your eyes and thank God you're learning this lesson, so you will never, never, ever! let ambition get the best of you.

b. Is it possible to own several companies?

When I sent this chapter to a friend -who owns several businesses, he replied: *"yes, it is possible"*. He gave me the examples of Carlos Slim –the richest man in the world; and Mesalles, a Costa Rican Tycoon with successful companies in many fields.

I acknowledge that my friend is highly disciplined, works hard, and has an above average intelligence that lets him *change tapes* successfully. So he has a point (and several companies!).

However...While there are people who create and successfully manage several companies at once, they are so exceptional as to prove the rule that one should not get into so many things. Furthermore, it is something that cannot be achieved overnight.

In the cases of billionaires like Slim or Mesalles, they have been in business for decades, have mentored managers and employees who have worked with them forever, becoming an efficient extension of themselves. They did not start ten companies in their first or second year. They have been through forty or fifty years as successful entrepreneurs.

Here I can also think of Warren Buffet, who along with Bill Gates and Slim, competes for the title of world's richest man. He owns -through his holding company Berkshire Hathaway, 63 companies (including a large portion of Coca-Cola, Johnson & Johnson & Procter and Gamble). How does he manage it? Every year he writes a letter to the CEOs of these companies, giving them goals for the year. He never holds meetings or calls them regularly. He just gives them two rules:

#1.You should not lose any money of the shareholders.

2.You should not forget rule # 1.

Tycoons create their many companies through several years in a process in which they form effective teams which become almost autonomous.

Remember: it is a process. Do not try to become a tycoon just after you do well in your first attempt.

This point is also related to diversification, and the fact that you should not put all your eggs in one basket. I did put all my eggs in the real estate market, the bubble burst, and, it was... It was not nice at all.

But diversification does not necessarily mean you need to have several companies. If you have savings in a bank or back-liquid investments outside your company, you are complying with the principle. The important thing is, if tomorrow something goes wrong with your business, you do not end up in the streets with no capital to start something different.

It does not mean you should have 10 companies in case things go wrong in nine. Moreover, I almost guarantee you that if you have ten companies; things will go wrong in nine!

c. Go slow, I am in haste...

As you have seen, now I talk wonders of my brother.

The truth is... I used to give him so much aggravation!

I always criticized him, because I thought he was *going too slow!*

Why don't you buy a Mercedes? You can! Nissan? Are you kidding me? You reinvest everything in your company? Come on! Yes, it is a good company, but you have to enjoy your money, don't you? One vacation per year? You could be traveling the world!

Remember the story of the hare and the tortoise?

I was the hare: clever, fast (at least I thought so), driving my brand new, *leased* BMW...

My brother was the tortoise: conservative, going step by step, thinking everything through, saving, reinvesting, driving around in his *completely paid for* Nissan...

Who do you think won this race? My brother not only won the race, but the right to be in my book as an example of how to do things right. Now in addition to a consolidated company, he has reserves. He could buy the Mercedes in cash if he wanted; although, as he says, he doesn't need to impress anybody.

Life teaches you so much! And that lesson we learned as children, that story of the hare and the tortoise, ends up being so true:

Sometimes, we try to run so fast that we can't see the dangers until we have them before us.

We don't see the tiger hiding in the trees until it is about to eat us.

Or we run pass the next opportunity without paying attention.

We are so focused thinking "*I have to get there, I have to win, I have to prove how successful I am*", that we don't think what we should be thinking: *What do I need in order to get there? Is this really the best way? What if I explore this other way?*

When we go calmly, we stop and ask for directions. We pay attention to the road. We even have the time to stop and help another little animal in distress. And maybe it gives us valuable advice. *"Don't take the shortcut, the tiger is there, he is waiting..."*

For many entrepreneurs before the recession, it was something like *"The housing market may collapse, this is not a good time to buy properties."*

What? When did they say that? But ... I just paid two million dollars for a property!

And the market fell. ***And the tiger ate me.***

Pinch by pinch you can kill an elephant. Or go slowly because I am in haste, as my grandfather used to say.

My grandparents were really wise! And so is my brother, who made time to stop and pay attention to them.

d. Beware of growing too fast

I just said that in life, it is better to be the wise turtle than the *"clever"* hare... All the lessons I just described, apply directly in business: when we are going too fast -blinded by the illusion of *quick profits,* we also tend to forget the foundations. And without them, eventually everything could crumble.

It is like a float, (ice cream with Coke). The foam rises rapidly to almost get out of the glass... However, after a while, it disappears and you realize the glass is half empty.

Sometimes a company that appears strong and successful from the outside truly is just that, bubbles...

Healthy growth in a company should be sufficient to keep it competitive.

"Growing" should not be the ultimate goal.

After all, the important thing is not to grow, but to make money!

Healthy growth does not happen in a day or a year. It is a long process that requires patience, so the growth is sustainable in the long term.

I read that Chinese entrepreneurs plan so they see profits in twenty years. I would personally go crazy.

My idea is to plan growth in cycles of seven years. There is something Kabbalistic with the number seven in all cultures. In the Bible, Joseph fat cows lasted seven years, and the drought also lasted seven years. Seven days it took God to make the world. Seven always mean the end, completeness ... But besides the Kabbalistic aspects... Years go by so fast!

The first three years are to lay the foundations and get to know the company; to define and test the products; to create a good team; to find reliable suppliers, to reduce cost-control to a science; to know which clients and customers we don't want, and to create a cash fund for emergencies.

For example, if you have a product or concept that is not fully tested, it is better to go slowly, testing, improving and eliminating errors, instead of massively selling something that may ultimately go bad or is more expensive than we thought.

In the U.S., companies often use limited markets or focus-groups to test the reactions of potential customers, get feedback and improve the product before making massive investments covering the country with something that may not meet expectations. If your product does not allow this; or you don't have the resources for this type of tool, the secret is to start slowly, and get feedback from customers as you go. You can't afford the mistake of jumping without a parachute with a product that, in the end, not even your grandmother likes.

The next four years of the cycle are for growing, step by step and carefully. It's like a marriage. According to statistics, if you are still married after seven years, the divorce figures drop dramatically! If you do not lay a firm foundation, it is almost certain that your company will not reach seven years, or if it does, it will be wrapped in debts, problems, demands and claims, until you can make the miracle of selling it or closing it.

Now, I understand that talking to entrepreneurs of patience, and cycles of 3 to 7 years, is almost like suggesting them to jab needles in the nails just for pleasure. Entrepreneurs are born with a virus that makes their blood boil: the **SOU Sense of Urgency.** It's a good virus, with symptoms that include the desire to move forward, to achieve goals, always going forward breaking any barriers that appear.

The problem is when it mutates into a rare disease: **ATA-Anxiety to Advance.** Our desire is transformed into anxiety to go faster than we should, without considering consequences... We want it all, and we want it *NOW!* We want the project to begin, the product to be sold, the company to be successful, the goal to be reached *immediately.* The disease manifests when we start getting what we want even if we have to skip processes, to jump steps, to go without a good plan, to ignore requirements, to demand results regardless of how they are achieved. However, time saved this way, has a strange way of getting back at you: sometimes *saving* a month cost you to lose a year, and you get in so much trouble!

Never allow the healthy desire to accomplish your goals to evolve into something negative that makes you lose perspective. I know it sounds like folly: **it is a process!** And as so, it has stages that can't be ignored.

There is also another truth on growing for the sake of growing: *the larger the company, the more difficult to control, to maneuver, to adjust the course*.

When personal computers came out, IBM was so, so big, that it was surpassed by competitors like Dell, which began in a garage at age 15!

Sometimes, it is better to keep small and clever like David, instead of being a not so smart giant like Goliath. Little David became king. But to go from a shepherd to be the most famous king in history, many, many years passed by and he needed lots of discipline.

Apple, at the beginning, faced imminent bankruptcy, a victim of its own success... Because they went so fast to try and sell a computer that was not ready, it became a fiasco, and we almost lost the company that gave us the IPhone and IPod. Although after reading Steve Jobs biography, and learn about everything he overcame, I have to say that if Apple would have gone bankrupt, Jobs would have learned his lesson and founded *Grape* a year later; and our computers would have a *little grape* and not an *apple*. Some are born to be great no matter the obstacles that life throws at them!

e. Beware of 'opportunities'

We said that when we have a certain level of success, many will approach us with business opportunities. Everyone has great ideas! Generally what they require from us is *'nothing more'* than money. One of the most important lessons to be learned as an entrepreneur is **when** to *miss* or *pass* on an opportunity.

Not all that glitters is gold.

Not all that looks like an opportunity is.

Ruin disguises as opportunity, because otherwise nobody would pursue it.

To learn how to distinguish between true and false opportunities ensures our success and prevents our fall. In real opportunities:

1. You are fully prepared for them. They are in a field that you know, in something you like and are passionate about, and you were looking for them.

2. You have the resources to do it, and you don't have to rush to borrow money or to mortgage your house or your other businesses. It is hard to learn the discipline I saw the other day when a friend turned down an opportunity that actually looked very good: *"Look, I know that the opportunity is excellent; BUT it is NOT my opportunity. I don't have the money to do it, and to get involved in it I will be committing all sorts of irresponsible acts. That opportunity is for somebody else that is better prepared than me'*

Something magical happens when we are responsible and don't tempt fate... The real opportunities will be there in the future when we are ready to take them...

Look at history. Your grandfather probably told you about the great opportunities that existed in his time. Or your father, did he ever tell you how he could have bought a property in the best area of town for cents of what it is today? And I am sure that Nero's cousins, in ancient Rome, found plenty of opportunities because they were the Emperor's family. So did Caligula's best friends (though, knowing Caligula, he probably had them '*disappear*')

It is part of the creating nature of this beautiful and expanding Universe; of a world that grows and improves every day. The terribly scarce resource is people really prepared to seize them.

However, there's nothing sadder than an opportunity turned into a curse because it was not our time, and we end up losing our shirts!

As a hopeless optimist I always used to advise people that opportunities had to be seized. '*Take risks. Do it because you may let 'your big one' pass by, and regret it for the rest of your life.*' Today, after a few blows that made me wiser, my advice is:

If there is something that seems like an 'opportunity', don't dismiss it; but don't take it on the air. Take your time, breathe deeply, and think it through...

If you need to come with money (and you usually do), is that money going to get you in trouble? If things don't go as you think, can this turn into a curse? ¿ Could the payments make your life miserable? What are you risking by taking this chance?

A couple of friends lost their house pursuing an *opportunity*. They lived in a nice condo worth $130.000, in a good area of town. They owed $60,000. Mortgage payment was $700, plus $250 in expenses (HOA, electricity, taxes, etc.) A total of $950 a month.

Then, they were offered an "opportunity". A house which would normally be worth $400,000, the owner had to *sell it now*, and was asking *just* $325,000.

Seemed like a great deal, with an *automatic profit*.. It also came with an approved loan, and no need for cash up front, as the seller accepted their condo —with equity of $70K, as down payment.

It sounds so good that you have to grab it on the air, right? That's what they thought. Their business was growing, things were good, and they felt ready to make the jump. Because it seemed so good, they did not sit down to make the numbers: the illusion of a big house made them forget they were not prepared.

The bank's payment was now $3000, plus $1000 of HOA, utilities and taxes. Therefore expenses went from $950 to $4,000 a month. And the interest rate —adjustable-, increased and expenses jumped to $5000. As if it was not bad enough, the market dropped, and if they sold the house, they barely could get $300,000. They ended up in foreclosure and lost it because they didn't find a buyer in time. Opportunity?

Beware of things that only *look* like it. Don't get too excited. It is not about making money and more money. That is vanity, an illusion. You have to relax and enjoy life. .Don't get me wrong: you have to grow and always have the ambition to go forward, because there is no such thing as 'being still'; you are either advancing or retreating. But play smart; be careful; develop your *nose* and be honest with yourself.

My friends made several mistakes. They broke the principle of budget, and did not calculate if they had the resources to proceed. Also, the principle of going step by step: they tried. to go faster than they could.

Time and opportunity reach everyone, but to identify real ones you must be prepared. If not, you will not seize -or distinguish- between opportunity and curse. So study, learn and exercise your brain. If you are interested in a topic, read all about that topic. Learn a new language. Learn a bit of accounting and numbers. Be ready. If you only learned about the color green, you will not be able to tell when opportunities present dressed in blue, white or red.

A note on Optimism (from an optimistic)

Optimism has at least two sides. One is great, and translates into the ability to face failure and setbacks thinking, 'ummm, I wonder what good will come out of this'.

After a failure, optimism let us use the debris of 'what was' as building blocks for what 'should be'. An optimistic believes in him/herself, and knows everything is possible to those who believe.

But it has a negative side: over optimism can blind us to realities. I.E., as we have seen, when crunching the numbers for a new business, we could tend to ignore hidden costs or potential problems, because we want it so badly to work!

Or we can underestimate a potentially damaging situation, or even, the effects of a crisis (remember 2007-8?)

We should be optimistic. I prefer that to being 'realistic' (those never do anything, because, well, it is 'impossible'. Airplanes? Those Wright brothers are just craaazy!)

However, we should seek balance, knowing that we can achieve anything we set our minds to, but keeping our eyes open to threats and paying attention to the environment. Listen to your heart, but also listen to traffic: you don´t want to miss that train coming right in your direction!

PRINCIPLES OF THE CHAPTER

• Take care of your business! Be there! If you concentrate all your energy in a venture, and don't make the mistakes mentioned throughout this book, you will succeed. However, if your attention splits into lots of things; or you try to have several companies when you are unprepared to handle them - without going through the process, failure will become a real possibility!

• Entrepreneurs with several successful companies have spent many years building them, training managers, testing them over and over. They have reduced the administration to procedures and manuals: they had made a science of it. Do not get into more things until you have reduced your business to a science; until you have spent years consolidating it. And yet, be careful.

• N*ot putting all your eggs in one basket,* does not mean to have several companies. It means to have liquid investments or savings besides your company, in case there is trouble or an attack of skinny cows.

• Greed kills; it creates stress and destroys happiness. How many rich people do you know that are so busy doing things they hate, that have no time for their wife, their children or their friends; or for a round of golf once in a while?

• Not all that glitters is gold. Curse disguises as Opportunity. Analyze each opportunity. Take your time. Don't rush. Never take an opportunity that is "just today." You are too old to believe that "*if you don't buy today, here, now, the offer is over.*" That is the first technique taught in timeshares sales! If they don't want you to think about it, there is a reason. Most probably, the reason is that if you actually analyze it, you will realize it would be foolish to do it.

• Think of the consequences! What if this is not exactly how it is being portrayed? What if this does not come out exactly as it is supposed to? Am you risking everything? Did you have to borrow it and pawn your shirt; or commit irresponsible acts; or fail to pay important things, so you can *"take it"*?

• Something magical happens when we are responsible and don't tempt fate. When we are brave to admit that we are not prepared. Fate will send us more opportunities when we are ready to say yes. Or better yet, know that they will be there waiting for you, because the Universe is a source of infinite opportunity.

• Prepare, study, learn ... That way you will expand the scope in which life can present options.

• Remember the hare, which seems faster and smarter, and the turtle -that goes slowly, and does not look as "cool". However the turtle has time to pay attention, ask for advice, understand what goes around, and make corrections in time.

• Do not use a successful company to *"save"* a *dead one* that you must have buried long ago. The dead are dead. Face it, cry it, bury it, and forget it.

PART THREE
The Other People

On friends, partners and employees

The naive believe everything, but the shrewd watch their steps." *Proverbs 14:15*

"In prosperity we cannot know our friends; in adversity an enemy will not remain concealed. When one is successful even an enemy is friendly; but in adversity even a friend disappears." *Sirach 12: 8-9*

First, a warning: No matter how good a person you are, or how many times a week you go to church, or if you help poor children, or even if you do good without looking to whom, know that there are bad people out there; people who want to take away what is yours.

In this life we must be careful and develop the capacity to identify the devourers, the scorpions. To learn how to defend what is ours!

Proverbs 6: 12-14 describes bad people. *"A wicked man (unworthy) is the one who walks with a perverse mouth (always walk with lies). Who winks with his eyes, who signals with his feet, who points with his fingers ... Who... continually devices evil, Who spread strife (always thinking of doing wrong, sowing discord, causing fights* say other versions)

When I read this, I immediately thought of a couple of people... And you probably did too!

The world of businesses is a jungle, where the naive and unsuspecting are devoured without mercy. We entrepreneurs are the most naive, because we are arrogant. We think we are so smart and know everything; so we don't investigate; do things in haste, and end up learning the hard way.

Now, it is not about walking through life *afraid*, it is about walking *prepared*. If you walk in the jungle with a GPS, a satellite phone, a lot of supplies, and a suit that repels snakes and wild animals, what is the problem? But if you walk naked thinking that snakes are pretty, that big spiders are like the ones in children books and tigers are just big cats, you're in trouble!

This part is about the principles and tools to go around the jungle, as the most experienced explorer.

LAW #5.
BE WISE WHEN CHOOSING FRIENDS, CLIENTS AND PARTNERS.

We said the world of business is a jungle where the naive and the trusting are eaten without mercy. The real problem is, we are terribly bad judges of character! As humans, we are easily manipulated and ultimately we want others to *like us* and to *accept us. And so we make so many mistakes in the name of 'love'!*

However, we said it is not about walking through life **afraid**, but **prepared**. And in business this means drafting good contracts; not trusting people and adjusting your radar. Trust your instincts: something within you will try to warn you when you are about to make a mistake. Call it Sixth Sense, Guardian Angel or Holy Spirit.

"But I need to make that sale... But I need that partner... But I have to impress those customers ... They look like very good people, and perhaps we even end up in a beautiful friendship...'

All I can say is:

In business, there are no friends! No one who is your counter party in a business has your best interest in mind. Not your partners, not your employees, not your clients... They all will seek to meet their own interests first.

They say a father told his son *"Son, let yourself fall back, I am here to hold you"* The child dropped, and the father allowed him to receive a tremendous blow against the floor. Sobbing, he asks, *'Father, why?'* And the answer was:

"So you learn to trust... no one!"

Generally, partners are looking for ways to get a higher percentage of shares for less money; clients are looking for a discount or better conditions... And to achieve that they will smile at you, invite you to a birthday party or to their little girl's first communion. Because they know that at a chosen day and time, you will feel you owe them something, and since you want to look good, you will give what your *'friends'*, *'comrades'*, and *'compadres'* want.

I'm not saying you will not meet interesting people with whom you could develop a business and personal relationship. However, those are exceptions, and you have to understand them as such. NEVER FORGET:

When the first problem arises in a contract, friendships disappear. When there is money involved, even families fight. There's nothing like the death of a rich relative without a will, for the real personalities to show. Now, imagine someone you just met in business!

a. Friends and Businesses

Friends and business are extremely difficult to mix and it usually ends up being fatal to friendship.

John Rockefeller summed up this principle in an extraordinary way *"I prefer one thousand times a friendship born from a business, than a business born from a friendship."*

At parties, in between sips of Tequila and laughing at jokes, we all seem so nice! However, in the midst of business, problems and money issues, the true personalities, the values, principles, and even the ability to remain calm and not shouting nonsense, will inevitably surface. So, don't base your business decisions in how much people laugh at your jokes, because I can assure you that you will not be the one laughing last.

Don't get me wrong. I'm not traumatized with life and think everybody is bad. Yes, I have taken hard blows for being a little over trusting, but more than that, for having neglected things and done them in haste, and for not stopping to analyze things in depth.

I firmly believe that there are good and reliable people out there, from whom we can learn, and it is our duty to find them. But as a principle, we must take great care when choosing partners, employees and even friends. The risk is enormous.

b. Choosing Partners.

A partner is *someone to whom we look for their ability to contribute in a potential deal, with something we lack. Call it money, contacts, ideas, office space, a talent or an exceptional ability... Something we need, and that person apparently has it and is willing to contribute it to a joint venture for the gain and profit of both."*

At first glance, it sounds pretty good. That person completes us. *You complete me,* as Jerry McGuire said in the movie. However, this definition does not even begin to describe the reality of what happens when people decide to join forces, talents or money towards an objective or goal.

1. Objectives of a partnership. A first problem that arises between partners is that **they don't necessarily have the same goal or objective in mind.** The following example illustrates this:

Maria bakes some really good cakes. She loves this and has always dreamed of baking cakes; it is her "purpose in life." Her weakness is sales. She does not know how to sell. Karla is a seller, she's one of those sales people you only watch on films, the kind that could sell umbrellas in the middle of drought.. One day, they meet at a party, begin to speak, and Eureka! Maria wants to bake cakes, Karla is out of work, and they are the perfect match. Right?

Let's see. Maria's goal is to fulfill her dream of making the best cakes in the world, so she can 'be happy'. But, what is Karla's goal? As the situation is hard and there are no jobs, selling cakes is a chance to earn some money and get by in the meantime. Ahhhh! Because it is in the *meantime...* When the real estate market improves, there is more money there...

You should always have your objectives –and those of your partner, CLEAR. Not necessarily the fact that they are different is an unsolvable problem. However, you need to know what to expect from the partnership.

In this case their goals are so different that as partners they will fail. For Mary, faithful to her purpose, she will put her heart and soul into the cakes. Karla in turn, will sell cakes while looking for properties to be ready when the market rises. The worst thing is that, she is a diabetic! She can't eat cake, so she can't even verify they are SO GOOD! She neither believes in the product nor does she care...

Karla and Maria should have not associated. As they were not careful to identify or question the goals they had in mind, now they are trapped in a complicated situation. And there is a final problem. They agreed that profits should be divided 50% - 50%. Karla understood it was 50-50% of the selling price of the cake, and Maria understood that the materials to make the cake must be subtracted. And they don't even have a contract... Farewell partnership. When this nightmare is over, they are never to speak to each other again.

I call this the Paradox of Different Objectives. It is a paradox they did not talk a little more before becoming partners...

2. When both partners contribute money. The rule in this case is,

Unless you have deep (and full) pockets, always choose partners who are at your same level or a little higher.

¿ Why?. Because when you need more money, -and always, always, more money will be needed, you need your partner to be in the same or better capacity than you to come with it. If you have a lot of money, no problem; but if neither of the partners does, and it is needed, what do you do? It is a mess!

This is the Paradox of the Broken-Broken... Either the business is broken, or the friendship is broken. If one ends up coming with the money, he will resent the other for not coming through *'at the time of trial'*. And the one who couldn't come with the money will resent the fact that the other now wants a higher percentage of shares. *"Wow, he is taking advantage!"*

3. When the contribution is a 'talent'. Here one partner doesn't contribute either money or ideas, but a "special talent", I.E. a great chef (for a restaurant), an excellent seller (for a business, like Maria and Karla's example), a great manager, or the best mechanic (for a workshop).

Yes, possibly having those people in your company can be excellent, and will bring benefits; but, do you really need a partner? ¿ Do you need someone to tell you what you can do or not do with your company? Someone to control your hours and get upset because you (who came with the money, the idea and even the place), arrived a little late to the office? Many times, the solution is to hire the talented person, and pay him well, instead of getting a bad partner.

When you come up with the money and the ideas, and your partner only provides a "talent", always analyze first whether it is best to hire him/her as an employee.

After all, if you make the Chef a partner, first, you still have to pay his/her salary; then, if there is something left, you have to share the profit with him. So, your *partner* is the only one who will always receive something, even if the business is not doing well. On the other hand, you, the one who came up with everything, become necessary only to pay bills or solve problems, but never to see profits!

c. Ideal partners

Relax... It is possible to have successful partnerships. The secret is to choose well and to remember that not all your friends, or those who you like, or those out there that look like good people, may be your partners. Remember what Rockefeller said.

In the next chapter I recommend you to be careful when seeking employees. Imagine how careful you need to be to find a partner!

Besides sharing your goals and objectives, the ideal partner should be:

1. *A counterweight; a balance.* If you "see the big picture", find a partner who is into details. If you are good in sales, but bad with numbers or control, find a partner who is organized in these aspects.

2. *A positive person* with similar values, from whom you are able to learn.

3. *An honest person,* somebody of principles. Run away from liars or those who break the law or bend the rules (they will breach the contract with you); or bad tempered or violent people.

Talk to your *candidates*. A fish dies because he opened the mouth. You will recognize a crook just by talking with him. He will say something, or tell you a story which will allow you to recognize his true self. Somebody I used to admire one day told me how he took advantage of a restaurant because of an error in their advertisement. He went with five friends, ordered expensive things, and finally, left the restaurant without paying thanks to that error. That made me question a lot of the positive things I believed of him. He didn't even considered to think about the restaurant owner, who maybe was struggling, having to "pay" employees and invoices...

4. *.In a similar financial condition* or only slightly superior. It is easier to deal with your peers than with someone who feels "better" than you. Be careful to partner with someone who is too high up from you, because the day that there is a problem, he might be able to crush you without mercy.

Besides, (and it happened to me once), since they have the money we need, and they know it, sometimes they ask for harsh conditions; to which, in our desperation to *"do business"* and because sometimes we are *"dazzled"* by their money and position, we don't pay attention or we don't pause to think in depth.

There is a clear warning in Shirach 13:2-4. *Bear no burden too heavy for you; go with no one greater or wealthier than yourself. How can the earthen pot go with the metal cauldron? When they knock together, the pot will be smashed. 4As long as the rich man can use you he will enslave you, but when you are exhausted, he will abandon you.*

However in this subject, as in everything in life, use common sense. If Bill Gates offers me to become his partner, I would forget the principle! (Maybe, he reads this book and thinks we can develop a program called "Microsoft Entrepreneurs". Bill, I'm available!)

When Wal-Mart arrived in Costa Rica, they offered to buy 51% of the largest supermarket chain. The owners would retain administration, but would have no "final" control. The option was to start competing head to head with the largest retail company in the world. They became partners.

Look into examples of modern corporations. In many companies the partners were good complements, which was the secret of their success. Bill Gates, who had great communication and social skills teamed up with Paul Allen, an excellent engineer and inventor. They were successful because they combined their skills. Steve Jobs also did well when he partnered with Steve Wozniak.

However, there are many stories of partnerships that didn't work, maybe because one stole the other's ideas; or one died and the other ended up dealing with nightmare heirs; or the partners were not compatible and ended up hating each other! Study those also; you will learn a lot. In conclusion,

When looking for a partner, start by defining what you want from him/her –the desirable personal characteristics; and the goals of the partnership. Perhaps you find them in a friend; perhaps you need to keep looking for a while.

It is always better to delay the start of a company than to trample yourself with the first person you found down the road. Going down on your face hurts; the first thing to hit the ground is your jaw...

d. Customers and clients

Every company needs time to build up a clientele, but more importantly, to get to know –and to choose, the customers and clients!

1. *You don't have to sell to everyone.* There are customers so problematic or so difficult, that they can ruin a business, and the worst thing you can do is to sell to them!

I once had a client who bought two houses from me. For three months she reviewed and questioned every single clause of the contract; every dot and comma... One day I got tired, and I found the courage to tell her *"I am sorry, but I will not sell to you!"*

She cried and promised me she was not going to be a problem. She acknowledged that she was maybe '*too detail oriented*' (she was on the diamond business; she cut diamonds for a living). Since she touched my big heart, I said *"well, okay, I'll build the houses for you."*

You know what happened? It was obvious from the beginning! She questioned every step of the construction! She rented another house at the project and spent months with my workers, measuring time after time every wall, window and door with diamond cutting precision. She made me knock down walls and rebuild them. We spend in those houses twice as much time, resources and money than in any other house. I lost money, and we –I and every single one of my workers- almost went crazy. And at the end, she was not pleased!

This terrible experience, taught me a great lesson. If a client creates problems from the start, from the contract, from the moment you are trying to sell, it will surely create problems half the road, three quarters, at the end... And then, they will sue you!

People do not change, even if they promise you otherwise!

Avoid the Pareto Law, in which 80% of your effort generates only 20% of your income. If your product is attracting a type of customer that you don't really want, change it! Maybe it just needs adjustments to attract a better clientele.

I must clarify that I also had excellent customers. They made reasonable requests in the contracts and paid on time. They loved the houses; never tried to find excuses for not paying; and even invited me for a glass of wine to celebrate when they moved in! I think I made my point.

2. The risk of selling on credit. You need time to study whether customers pay or don´t pay; or even if they pay, whether they take a long time.

This is a cost entrepreneurs forget to consider: sometimes you have to borrow to cover such deferred payments; or even to discount accounts receivables for cash flow. I understand this takes time; changes in strategies. But if within six months you are a giant and sold everything on credit, -only to discover that your customers don't pay, now what?

Another thing you need to determine is whether your clients are affected by cyclical factors (like in most businesses). In the first year you will not know even if there are "cycles".

3. Listen to your clients! Now days, companies are created or destroyed on the internet. A good or bad recommendation on Yelp or Angie's list could be crucial. You have to be aware whether the clients are praising or criticizing your product. Bill Gates said that "Your most unhappy customers are your greatest source of learning." Pay attention and make the necessary corrections. One client spreading rumors or critics against you in blogs could make potential clients think twice about you. However, what if he/she is right?

PRINCIPLES OF THE CHAPTER

• Good partners are like diamonds... Scarce!

• Bad partners are like diamonds... Expensive!

• If you are naive and believe that tigers are just big furry cats, they'll eat you. If you walk prepared and protect yourself, it will be all right; but if you trust everybody...

• Do not believe in appearances. People who want to steal your money will not come disguised as bank robbers. They will look serious, trustworthy and friendly.

• Beware of anyone who offers friendship while doing business. They will invite you to birthdays, first communions and even church, providing there is a deal in which they could obtain some benefit.

• In a partner we look for something we need and we don't have. The partner *apparently* has it and is willing to contribute it to a joint venture for the gain and profit of both. I say *"apparently"* because it is not always true that they have what they *"offer"*. And if you don't research well, don't ask the right questions, or don't have a good contract, you may end up with a partner who lied, who contributed nothing, and now you are stuck for who knows how long!

• Before partnering with somebody for their talents (a chef, a manager, or mechanic), no matter how good it is, consider first hiring them. Do you want to pay them a salary, give them 50% of the profits; and still have 100% of the risk?

• And remember, it is better to lose a sale or a client, than to lose a lot of money, and time, and life! There are bad clients. Identify them and run!

LAW #6
CHOOSE YOUR EMPLOYEES CAREFULLY.

With employees, it applies almost all of the same principles as with partners, including the principle that:

Good employees are like diamonds... Scarce!

Bad employees are like diamonds... Expensive!

Bad employees can ruin a company. A resentful one, especially with access to sensitive information can tear up a big corporation.. It is really difficult to meet 100% of all laws, regulations, licenses, taxes, and anything politicians create. Therefore, an employee has an almost innate ability to get the Government touching at your door in no time, even if based on lies!

So, if we know they have so much power, why do we hire the first son of neighbor who approaches us with a story of sadness and asks us for a job?

It was so hard for me to understand this!

My wife, who has proven to be smarter than me on some things (I say *some* things because if I don't clarify she will use it against me!), has always been light years ahead of me on this subject.

For her business, she would place an ad in the newspaper and. on line, receive up to 100 resumes, check them one by one, and pull the top 10. She would recheck, choose the best five, call the references and check if they were real or relevant (she caught a few false numbers!). Then, she would call them for an interview, and for a half hour, ask all kind of questions.

So tell me about your mother... (She thinks that sons of strong women will work well with a strong female leader. Interesting theory!)

Are you married? Do you have children? (To determine how stable his/her environment)

What school did you attend? Why did you last eight years in college, instead of four? (To determine whether it was because he/she was dumb or because he/she had to work and support five brothers, and study only at night, which is rather admirable).

Why did you leave your last job? Tell me about your previous employers (if an employee speaks ill of the last boss, the day they leave your company they will speak ill of you!)

.From the final five, she would pick three for a second interview; and then, finally, choose the ideal one.

Only once I can say that she was wrong, and I think it was because she asked for my opinion, ha!

But usually, she hired honest people who did a good job. People who left the company because they got offered a better position, often with double the pay. In other words, she had chosen well...

Me, on the other hand ... I'm embarrassed to even remember.

"Mr. Chaves, *John's cousin is unemployed and is in need... Do you think there could be an opening for him? He is smart and hardworking...*"

"*Well, we may need someone in administration. Does he know anything about that?*"

"*I think so. He is a very good person. And I've seen him using computers.*"

"*Well, okay, I'll give him a try; tell him to come on Monday...*"

And two months later I had to fire him because he had stolen supplies, after wasting precious time training him because he could not do anything: he was half dumb-half lazy, and the only computer he had ever used was a PlayStation. And after that, he asked for 'severance payment', and bad-mouthed the company... and ME!!!

.The last mistake I made was when I hired a collector to pick up payments. Since I had no time for the interviewing process, and it was urgent, I let my assistant do it. And we ended up hiring an employee's second cousin. The first day - THE VERY FIRST DAY, he was "mugged" and somebody stole $1000 in cash that he had collected from a client (they mostly paid by checks. He was "mugged" the day one paid in cash!) And how could we prove it was auto-theft? I barely knew his name! In retrospect, the half dumb-half lazy one was me. Not anymore!

Now, in my defense, what happened to me happens to so many! And it is so very seriously wrong. It costs not only money, but the image of the company!

Bad employees reflect poorly on your business. People never say '*that employee treated me badly*'; they say '*that company treated me badly and I would never buy from them again'.* Or *'Southwest Airlines didn't let me board because I supposedly was too fat, so, let's boycott the airline',* instead of saying *'some fool came out with this explanation, and didn't know I was a well-known Hollywood director whose case was going to be all over the news"* as happened a few years back to Kevin Smith.

Bad employees take time and productivity from other employees, not just because they have to be trained, or because things have to be done twice, but because they waste time commenting that the boss (you!) does not know how to choose people for the company.

They cost *your* time, as you have to spend hours attending complaints, or just fixing problems caused by their inefficiency, lack of intelligence or ill will.

And all because of the damn laziness!

In. the end, it *is* laziness. Sadly, our culture is not one of excellence. We want everything fast and easy. Instant meals, instant pleasure, instant gratification.

It does not work that way with employees!

You may have read in fifty books that **the key to a company's success is a good team.** I repeat it in case you didn't understand: a successful business is the result of a good group of employees. And a company with bad employees, no matter if it sells the best product in the world, will end up closing.

I had bad employees. Employees who robbed me blind; or even one that planned a robbery on one of my buildings to steal the appliances; others that constantly used "sick" days; or some that were like "furniture" - those who do the same function as an empty chair, they are "there" but do nothing.

However, I also had the blessing of outstanding employees -those hired by luck or by simple law of probabilities, to which I gave neither the place nor the attention they deserved, and who ended up moving to other companies where they were duly appreciated.

.As an employer, you have an exceptional task. .If you want your company to be successful, take the time required to build a good team. Every minute spent on this process, will save you hours of problems and several headaches.

There are dozens of human resources books available. The following are some simple rules:

a. Define the requirements of the position. Don't hire somebody, and then look for something for him/her to do. People do this a lot, to hire employees without knowing exactly what they need them for.

b. Place ads. Whether yours is a huge undertaking or a hot dogs stand, receive multiple resumes or candidates for the position. If out of courtesy you interview the cousin of a friend of your secretary's brother, treat them like any other candidate in equal conditions.

c. Develop your instinct to find honest people (you will understand when you read the next chapter)

d. Do not settle for less. If you didn't get the candidate you want, place a new ad. Do not hire the "*second best*"; you want **the best.** If you insist, you are likely to find it. If your business is important to you, the person whom you bring in has to be as important. My wife always managed to find the ideal candidate. But she was not lazy, and if she had to place an ad two or three times, she would do it.

.**e. Try them.** People would give three months to test an employee. But why wait so long? If it didn't work in the first month, don't waste time. It won't work. Why spend time and energy in someone who could not comply with the saying "any new broom sweeps clean." A new employee should give you his best: he should be trying to impress everybody. He is fresh and supposedly has not developed 'tricks' yet. If it doesn't work in the first month, **it won't work.** Fire him/her and place a new ad.

d. **Evaluate them constantly.** Never let your employees feel so comfortable that it seems you no longer care. Challenge them, keep them alert. Show them that since you hired the best, you expect the best. If they are doing a good job, tell them. And if not, all the more reasons to tell them!

If you took the time to do all this, you will probably form a good team, and they will thank you.

HOWEVER, NEVER make the mistake of putting a bad employee into a good group. The saying *'one bad apple rots the whole bag'* is true! Too bad we do not pay attention. If you have a good team, and hire a disloyal employee who loses time, who doesn't do his job, who is a gossip or is problematic; and you do nothing about it, your good employees will quit, because they will not stand working with someone like that; or they will simply lose interest and become like the bad employee: *if the boss doesn't care, me neither.*

Be very careful about who gets in your company.

If you hire a thief, he / she is going to steal!

If you hire a bum, he/ she is not going to work, and will make others not to work!

If you hire a gossip, soon everyone will walk in gossip.

If you hire a revolutionary, he or she will organize all into seeing you as the enemy.

If you plant a pear tree, you will get pears.

Or did you believe that the rules of life do not apply to you anymore, just because you are "**an entrepreneur**"?

PRINCIPLES OF THE CHAPTER

•You must make an effort to hire the best employees. Investing the necessary time in creating a good team is the foundation for your success or failure. I know you're busy. But however busy, never make exceptions to the rule of being careful when hiring, or you'll be many times sorry. If you bring a bad apple into a good team, it will rot the whole bag. And if they don't rot, they will run away.

•There are six sacred steps: Define the position, place the ad, receive applications, do interviews, hire the best, and test them. If is not working within a month, fire them immediately and start again.

•The best employee I had -and I had no less than five hundred, was Victor. I hired him by chance as he was the cousin of another employee. Yes, I know! I know! Anyway, in this case it worked. That guy had a good attitude from day one. Always smiling. All the other employees and the customers respected him and loved him, for he had a special charisma. He worked super hard, always working and working. He was always available. However, due to my 'occupations' I never took time to thank him or to become his mentor. I lost him when I closed that company (he even worked without pay for a few days). If you ever find Victors in your business, take care of them as treasures. Pay them well. Encourage them, give them opportunities. Those are the ones to look for.

LAW #7.
PUT EVERYTHING IN WRITING!

Never, never, NEVER! do any type of business that involves money, any deal, any commitment, VERBALLY!

Not even with the holiest of men!

Always, always, ALWAYS! Put everything in writing.

a. Little papers do talk.

You could have the best product or best idea in the world - something you know is going to make you happy and to which you will give your maximum effort. You could have crunched the number realistically and you are ready to make money... But if your contracts are weak, **you are doomed!**

But we are such good friends...

But he's my cousin!

But if I cannot trust this person, who could I trust?

The principle of **everything must go in writing**, goes beyond trust; or if your counterparty is a good person; or whether people act in good or bad faith.

The problem here is that money - no matter the amount-, causes STA. STA is a very serious syndrome behind most broken friendships, severed family ties, and former best friends that hate each other. It is the worst disease that attacks the careless entrepreneur...

STA - Selective Temporary Amnesia: In any business arrangement made verbally, people remember only what is in their best interest.

So, what happens when you make a verbal agreement with someone?

Let's go back to the hot dogs business, and assume you decide to do business with your friend Mark. As the business is so simple, you just sit and talk. *"So you do this, I do that, and in the end, we split the profits. Agreed? Of course!"* And you shook hands with a smile, because you are a person of your word, and you are sure your friend is also! And you start the business.

What happens to 99% of business made this way? Let's see. You had to work more than agreed (or so you think), because Mark didn't do what he said he would do. Because he said it, *so you remember*, right? He'd had to do some things and he didn't.

And when the time for profit distribution arrives (if it does!) ... a never ending fight starts. If you said or said not; or if you did or did not; *but I thought; but I assumed, but I am sure that was what you meant,* and so on so forth!

"What? Are you deducting the gasoline from my part? Are you crazy? That is on your part, remember ... No? ... But you said so!

The worst thing is that if somebody asks your former 'friend' about what just happened, he is going to say *'No! That guy is horrible. He made up all these things at the end! And I am the one that had to work harder, because he never did anything. And could you believe he wanted to deduct his gas from my profits!'*

So, who was right? **BOTH! AND NO ONE!**

Don't be fooled into thinking that you are completely right and own the ultimate truth. You are also remembering only **what suits you!**

It happens as when you are introduced to people. You are so interested in saying your own name, that you don't pay attention to the others'. They said it, but you can't remember it. Neither can the other person!

'But I told you that the gasoline was to be deducted' 'Never! You never told that. That's a Lie!'

'We agreed you would work Mondays and Wednesdays'

'No! No! I clearly said Mondays and **Thursdays**.. On Wednesdays I go to my girlfriend's house. You know that, she is YOUR SISTER!'

This is what happens when you enter into any kind of verbal contract or agreement. STA combined with the fact that we only remember what suits us. And it happens to us as much as to the others. That's why courts require two witnesses; because people always see or hear or understand only part of the truth.

Always, always, write down everything. ALL IN WRITTING. TODO POR ESCRITO. TUTTO SCRITTO. And if I knew how to say it in Chinese, I would write it. (According to google is: 所有书面. Hopefully I did not write a terrible insult, like in the movies.)

When my daughter was four years old, she learned a phrase that is famous in our family. '**Little papers DO TALK.**

'At what time will you come home, Mommy?'

'At Four'.

'Could you sign this little piece of paper that says you come back at four? Thank you'

Write it all down! *So gasoline is deducted from profits?* Yes it is deducted, it is a cost. *All right. And you work Mondays and Wednesdays? Oh no, it is true, Wednesday's you go to my sister's! Thursdays then! And I get 50% after we deduct what expenses exactly? What if we fight? What if we don't sell everything? What if this happens? What if that happens? And what if your sister and I break up?"*

There are people doing deals involving millions with a one page contract, and then complaining they had to waste years in courts!

If you don't want to waste years in court, arguing nonsense, Why not to spend one afternoon and sit down with your partner to do an in-depth analysis?

Think of all the possible consequences of the undertaking that begins.

You might even discover potential problems that had not occurred to either of you. Or new opportunities!

It is such a huge mistake made on all levels. We are so interested in doing it quickly, in starting to make money, or in making the deal happen, that we don't think in the business or in its consequences, or in what happens if Jenny does not pay the hot dogs we left her to sell, or if the car crashed while you were buying bread for the hot dogs (Do you pay the insurance deductible from the profits?)

b. Make your contracts as broad as possible.

Always, always, ALWAYS, write the contracts providing for all possibilities: all the good things that can happen; all the bad things that can happen. Think! Invest some time on this. 95% of the potential problems will go *away*.

'You told me Wednesdays!'

No, here in writing says Thursdays'

What do you think your partner will say? That you forged his signature? No! He would say: *"Oops, it is true ... Sorry!"*

People will remember! Even if they don't agree, it is there and it is signed.

'We said the fine for late delivery applies only if you paid on time. You didn't pay on time, so, no fine. It says here in the contract.

It says here that the house has only one closet in the master bedroom. I never said two closets'

This was the hardest lessons I learned as a real estate developer. My contracts were so simple, so *'nice' (so weak!)* that people, -some of them good people- ended up taking advantage. Whose fault was that? MINE! I did not write good contracts! I did not invest enough time and energy in contracts that would protect me from *'misunderstandings'*.

Most contracts in the U.S. are hundreds of pages long. They have everything. Try suing somebody. Try collecting your insurance *'Sorry, according to clause seven hundred and ninety, paragraph 35, in relation to clause fourth of addendum number five, your claim is specifically excluded. And see, your signature is there, next to it, you almost signed over it.'*

We could avoid so many problems if we would made better contracts and get used to writing everything. You probably would still have some of the friends you no longer have. And you would still be speaking to your brother in law... And more importantly, that business that once gave you so much hope, would have not become a nightmare, and would have not cost you so much pain, aggravation and MONEY!

PRINCIPLES OF THE CHAPTER

• ALWAYS, ALWAYS! put all agreements, *absolutely all agreements,* in writing.

• When in doubt, remember the above principle...

• ...Then, write it all!

• Everyone, *including you,* suffers Selective Temporary Amnesia, STA. You remember only what is in your best interest.. So does your partner! And if things are not in writing, the problems begin.

• People leave out of the contracts many scenarios of problems, sometimes for fear that the business falls apart or the potential partner panics. This is nonsense, because in the end, Murphy's Law applies. If the problem can happen, it will. And if the contract says nothing, it could become a never ending legal battle.

• Do as big corporations do. Protect yourself with long contracts, including everything and providing for anything that can go wrong. That reduces exponentially the likelihood of someone wanting to sue or take advantage of you. Is it a drag? Yes, but it is worst to visit courts and lawyers ... They´re expensive! Remember, laziness -our tendency to give the minimal effort in everything, especially when making decisions, leads to failure.

• Whether the business is with your cousin, with your best friend, the neighbor next door, or the man who sells you ice cream, if you want to keep the relationship, write absolutely everything and have everything clear. **Do not assume** that the other listened; or that you said or not said.. **Assumption is the mother of all screw-ups!**

• If your partner gets angry because you want to put things in writing, remember: it is better that he gets angry, rather than you losing money, work or effort; or developing an ulcer because of the annoyances. If you explain and show this book to him or her, perhaps they will understand that it is for the benefit of all.

• To be careful, to be entirely clear, and to ask everybody to put everything in writing, -and sign it, also can free you from Scammers. Scammers always want everything done fast, they don't want to give explanations, and if asked a lot of detail, generally make mistakes and fall into contradictions. Also, when someone is "nosy" or wants to be very specific, they prefer to run away. Scammers know that the world is full of careless, lazy, people that don't read contracts. People that would let themselves be pressured into the lie that the opportunity is only *today*, that the deal *has to be done. NOW, FAST!* If they see that you are not one of those, they will rather seek an easier victim.

LAW #8.
CONTROL, CONTROL,
¡CONTROL!

"He who neglects his house will inherit wind" (another
version says, *"nothing remains"*).

a. Theft is a BIG problem for companies.

As I confessed in the last chapter, a big mistake I made as
entrepreneur was to be over trusting.

I was raised with strict values regarding theft, and I pride
myself on being an honest person -I return the money when I
am given more change, or I seek the owner when I find
something. Therefore, in my companies, I made the mistake of
thinking that people had been educated in the same way.

We tend to think it s a sin to judge others; that if we have
negative thoughts about the others, God will judge us. But that
can make us fall into the trap of lowering the guard and making
ourselves vulnerable to others, which, as we saw in previous
chapters, is a near-fatal mistake.

I read that the main problem faced by large corporations in
the U.S. (and probably even worse in other countries), is theft.
Given the right circumstances, 90% (NINETY PERCENT) of
people will perpetrate some kind of theft on the companies they
work for. Only 10%, for reasons of education, religion and / or
personal values will not do it under any circumstances.

This does not mean employees spend their time planning a 'major coup'. To steal doesn't mean just to walk out the front door with a bag full of money.

It means missing work; taking excessive hours to go to the doctor; not reporting 'vacation days'. It means using the copier for personal things (the boss has lots of money and nobody is going to notice anyway); or pass the hours updating Facebook, instead of working. And doing it while thinking it is okay or *the way things are done...*

Obviously -and unfortunately, there are also real thieves. It's sad, because it's hard to believe that there are people who are consciously willing to steal. And much less to us, such good people that give all to our employees, treat them well, teach them... *Right?*

The other day, reading the Gospel of John (which I finished reading for the first time!), I found a quote that made me laugh, but got me thinking on this issue (so much I wrote this chapter, the first of this book)

Jesus was undoubtedly the nicest businessman that ever lived. He spent the days teaching his disciples. They were never in need, because if there was no food or wine, the "boss" provided (as in the multiplication of bread or the wine at Cana's wedding); and the retirement plan after life employment included *eternal life.*

How many of us wouldn't have accepted the job?

And yet, while enjoying all these privileges, among Jesus' *'employees'* there was a thief!

John tells a story of the infamous Judas, which is no doubt the example of the 'BAD EMPLOYEE' that all of us have had in our businesses. When Mary anointed Jesus' feet with expensive perfume, Judas complained that it should have been sold and delivered to the poor." And John 12:6 *says: "Now he said this not because he was concerned about the poor, but because he was a thief, and as he had the money box, he used to pilfer what was put into it."*

Unbelievable! Judas, worked for the best company; had the best retirement plan (eternal life); received free education (a permanent scholarship to learn from the great teacher); had free business lunches and dinners (they were constantly invited to homes); had the best health plan (you never heard of sick apostles; Jesus healed even those he met on the road).. In other words, Judas had all the benefits that an employee can enjoy.

And yet he was stealing!

Obviously, Jesus knew that Judas was stealing and would betray him. He let this happen, so the teaching and the principle remained. It was not because he thought '*Poor Judas. His kids are skinny and he needs cash to feed them*'. No! Jesus was thinking in leaving a lesson to all of us entrepreneurs, the ones who employ people, so we should be careful and think:

'*If they stole from Jesus, imagine what they would do to me!*' So...

b. Control, control, control!

How boring is to establish controls! It takes a lot of time.

Employees may think I'm a crazy control freak. And I'm really so nice! And all my people are so nice; I really don't think I need this...'

Don't be so naïve! You must do it! Or next time you check, there will be new TVs, new dining rooms new refrigerators, and new cars AT YOUR EMPLOYEES' HOUSES!

Remember what the father told his son in the story? **Trust... NO ONE!** Sounds harsh, because we know there are good people out there full of good intentions. However, if you want your company to last, you have to do like the dad. **90%** of people will find some mental justification to violate the seventh commandment: *DO NOT STEAL*. The odds are clearly against you. Do you know what the worst part is? That if you ask them, most don't even believe they're stealing!

It is important to have good controls. If they are supposed to use 100 units of something a day, and they are using 120, 20 are being stolen, NO DOUBT about it! Even worst if they handle cash! The idea is to make it as difficult as you can. At least make them think. If you make it easy, even 'good people' will fall into temptation. Guaranteed!

Remember Adam and Eve? They took a risk with the apple, because they thought there were no cameras in the Garden of Eden. The three had no fences around; and nobody seemed to be making a weekly report of how many apples were there. It seemed easy. Yes; they were warned; they were told not to do it! *'But God has many trees and apples. And the truth is, if I don't eat those delicious and juicy apples, they will probably fall and rot. Moreover, God doesn't really need them for anything, right?*

See, this is exactly how your employees justify themselves when taking something from you!

And although they have been told *"don't do it, it is not good"*, since there are no consequences and they probably won't get caught, they do it anyway, right?

But Adam and Eve didn't know that. God had installed safety devices. Or do you think God was like us, half-witted entrepreneurs? NO! The moment they grabbed the apple and ate it, BUUUUM! Their clothes were gone. They were discovered.

I bet that an alarm sounded in heaven and the celestial accountant came to report "Sorry, Mister God, I am sorry to bother you, is about little Adam and Miss Eve, they seem as such good kids, but look, according to this report, an apple is kind of missing!"

ESTABLISH CONTROLS! A good accountant is fundamental; but a vicious one! A friend suggested me to hire accountants with no social skills, hopefully NOSY, whose pulse will not shake when they have to go after Little Adam or Miss Eve, or Henry or Janin. And on top of the accountant, have a comptroller; because sometimes, *it is the accountant who steals!*

If you don't put in place the necessary controls - if your bad employees feel they can get away with it, they will find a thousand ways of stealing. If they robbed Jesus, they are definitely going to rob you. HAVE NO ILLUSIONS. The creativity of human beings, for better or for worse, is infinite. Even if you can't avoid all possible scenarios, at least MAKE IT HARD!

And give a copy of this chapter to your employees, so they know that at least you are concerned with the subject. If they are on the 10% they will laugh about it. However, if they belong to the 90%...

c. Remove the cancer

So, you caught the thief. It was Johnny in Procurement. Or worst, young Annie the cashier. *'Poor girl. She has children. And if I let her go, poor thing'*

In most Latin-American countries, people are so *nice*. So, we say, *poor people,* right? NO! POOR YOU!

And poor the next guy who hires him or her, when -after they steal again from you (if you forgive them, they will do it AGAIN), you finally fire them, and don't file the criminal complaint.

Do yourself a favor, and fire any employee who steals even something small. It is like a cancer: it starts small. The cancer starts in a cell that goes crazy and degenerates. Then, there are two, then ten, and when the body is completely invaded, the person dies.

How is someone saved from cancer? When cancer cells are detected in time, they are completely removed to the root, and the body regenerates. And then, the body is checked continuously to ensure no re-emergence.

If you have a business and want to still have it in ten years, REMOVE THE CANCERS.

Sometimes, we KNOW an employee is stealing. However, after making the calculations we say 'If I fire this person, I have to train somebody else, waste a lot of time, possibly even pay severance payment or go to court... *It will be more expensive than to just turn a blind eye.'*

FALSE! This cancer will grow. Because if you noticed, be sure that other employees noticed. And if they see you doing nothing, it is like shouting "opened cash register". And when you realize it, they leave you with nothing!

Fire any employee who steals, and be clear with others on why you did it.

Make them realize that you have your pants (or skirts!) on.

Let them know that if they try, there will be consequences!

If not, your employees will end up with a new house and a big TV, and you will end up with no company and still paying the mortgage on your house.

Don't forgive *their sins*. Fire them, remove them as a cancer and throw them out as God did with Adam in paradise. No letter of recommendation. No mercy!

You would not let a cancer cell thrive in your body, because you know that it will eventually kill you.

PRINCIPLES OF THE CHAPTER

• If Judas stole from Jesus, imagine what they are doing to you.

• 90% of employees, given the right circumstances, steal. In time, photocopies, or worse, IN CASH ... It is up to you to make it easy or make it difficult.

• Beware of employees who are always praising you (K.A.) and trying to fit right...Those are the worst!

• Trust no one. Set all kind of controls. If it walks like a duck, sounds like a duck and looks like a duck is a duck. Don't be fooled. If it looks like they are stealing from you *THEY ARE!* Where there's smoke there's fire. When the river makes sounds, it is carrying stones... This river is taking your stones to *his house!*

• Do not forgive a bad employee under any circumstances. I know you are a good person, and you believe in second chances, right? Forget about it! Did God give a second chance to Adam and Eve? They stole the apple, out they go. Everyone has to assume responsibility for their actions. An employee who steals is a cancer. If not removed, it will spread and, sooner or later, IT WILL KILL YOU!

• There are lots of good people out there. Your goal is to do well in the recruitment process, trying to hire people from the 10% who would never steal by education or principles. That is 700 million worldwide!

Note. I understand you are busy, therefore, my recommendation is not that you become obsessed with "employee stealing" and chain yourself to the cash register. There is also the law of attraction, and whatever becomes your dominant thought, happens. But consider this "knowledge" and take precautions. It will happen one way or another, is part of the cost of doing business, your task is to minimize it and its impact on your bottom line.

LAW #9.
COMMUNICATE
EFFECTIVELY

(And Shut Up Often!)

a. Do not talk more than you should.

'Everyone reaps the fruit of what he says' *Prov. 12:14*

'He that speaks much, much errs; silence is wise time' ***Prov. 10:19***

He who speaks too much will ruin itself.' ***Prov. 13:3***

"Life and death depend on the tongue." *Prov. 18:21*

Those who speak much suffer the consequences "***Prov. 10:20***

Those who speak, don't know. Those who know, don't speak. *Tao Te Ching.*

"Shut up and listen!" My Grandma

These are just a few of the many proverbs on this principle. Yesterday, today and forever, smart people have recognized how dangerous it is to talk more than necessary! And that wise people speak less!

Analyze your life for a second. How many times, when you have talked more than you should, there has been a benefit? Let's say you told a secret to a friend *(but you can't tell anyone,* you said) and your friend told another friend and the friend to another friend. What happened? Did anyone come back to you with a good proposal, because they heard you had a great plan? Or instead, you got into a mess, because someone heard fifth-hand that you said that so-and-so had told someone, that Mary told something to Peter?

They say you can't ask your friends to keep a secret when you were not able to hold back and keep the secret yourself. Why to ask others what you can't do?

I know people who simply can't keep anything to themselves. Especially after Twitter! 'I *just went into the bank, the wait is really long' 'I saw Mary at the supermarket'*. Really? Who cares! That Twitter thing drives me crazy! I have not opened an account or declared myself a follower of anyone. Actually, I could not care less if they saw Mary, or if the line was long at the Bank... I just find it incredible that people have so much time to waste!

b. Do not become a professional communicator of your life

In this life it is important to handle things with discretion, and not to become professional communicators of our lives and circumstances. There is a phrase that we see on TV when they arrest a criminal and read his rights. 'Anything you say can and will be used against you.' Most, apparently, have never being read their rights, because they tell everybody things that can and ARE used against them. Especially if they published it in Facebook!

Entrepreneurs are no exception. In Chapter 11, I beg you to, -if in trouble- not to tell everybody! The last thing you need is for your customers and suppliers to be scared because you talked too much with an acquaintance you found at the supermarket, and told him that your company was doing 'so-so' and that your cash flow was tight. Remember:

Anything you say can and will be used against you in the court of life.

It is true that sometimes we feel the need to share our success with others, or in times of challenge, to seek motivation or words of encouragement. Author and speaker **David Sariñana** –a personal friend, says in his book **"Vision for success"**, that we must be very careful in what we share with people. Whatever it is -dreams, goals, problems, not everyone will understand us or will care about it.

If we share our success, very few will be happy. Most will be jealous, and feel threatened. Some will even try to stop us with words and sometimes with actions. You have to identify them and stay away from these people, as they are dangerous and toxic for your life. These are the ones that when you face challenges, will administer the *coup de grace*.

If you want motivation, look for people who are moving forward. Only visionaries understand visionaries. They are on the same path, on the same journey, only ahead of you. That is the people that will give you encouragement and motivation.

c. Work on your image and your ability to communicate

In society you are exposed to be watched, judged, talked about and criticized. So you have to be very careful in the image you communicate.

Most successful people have understood how important it is to learn how to communicate, how to say what you mean, and how to convey ideas appropriately. Poor communication is not just talk more than necessary. It also occurs when what is said is not meant or when others don't understand or misunderstand what was said.

"I didn't mean it..."

But you said it!

Often problems arise because we don't control the gestures, tone of voice or words. It is not only about what is said but how it is said. Most divorces happen because of miscommunication.

Inmates have the lowest level of vocabulary in society. It is said that they commit crimes because they cannot communicate or communicate what they feel!

It is not only about living with integrity, but learning to communicate integrity, because communication is not limited to talk: 90% is nonverbal. The gestures, tone, the way you dress, convey much more than anything that is said. We live in a world where image counts, a world in which what you project externally is a fundamental key to success. There are smart people who could be successful, but come to meetings poorly dressed and disheveled, and their partners don't take them seriously because they think "if you cannot take care of yourself, you are not a reliable person"

To develop good communication skills, there are certain fundamental issues which should work.

1. Develop Self-esteem. If you are a confident person, you can talk to people without fear and do well in any environment. But if you are insecure and shy, you would not want to talk, will lower you head, and some will feel you are hiding something, because not all understand it's a communication problem.

Many, out of shyness, seem rude.

Also, there always comes a time when we have to "sell" our image, product or service to an audience that will decide whether to buy from us or someone else. Be careful with this: the chances and great opportunities will pass you by, if you are shy and don't show what you have.

A successful entrepreneur has to work hard in its self-esteem. Do you know who was the greatest inventor ever? An employee of Thomas Edison named Nicola Tesla. Most people don't even know his name, because he was shy and didn't know how to sell his ideas. When Edison discovered him, he made millions at his expense. Tesla instead ... It's sad.

By contrast, the man who invented the BIC ball pen, Biro, was a very likeable Hungarian journalist who believed in himself. After interviewing the President of Argentina in the late 40s, he convinced him to fund his inventions!

2. Learn to listen and show interest in others.
Have you noticed that we have one mouth but two ears? Learn to listen. We are quick to say what we want but don't listen to others.

If you did not listen to your employees when they try to explain the problems of the company, you can't provide solutions to those problems that you have neither heard nor understood. We could find many answers if we just would learn to listen!

You have eyes to observe and analyze people; ears to listen; a voice to express yourself; and hands and gestures to complement. Develop all your senses, not just the tongue.

Men are impatient. We want people to go to the point, not to be told every single detail, because we have no time to hear their stories. But that is how we miss the details. And in the details, many times, is the answer. Women have an advantage in this subject. Sometimes they not only listen to you, but they listen to the conversation at the next table, and have time to remember your shoes were dirty. *My wife does!*

But it's not just about listening; it is about demonstrating interest in others. What kind of things interest to the person you have in front of you? Where did he or she go to school? Ask for their children, their family. People like to feel special and important.

There are successful people who are like magnets, not because they are the smarter or the *most beautiful*, but because they transmit positive energy, are courteous, greet with a smile and say nice things. And as they make everybody feel good, all the doors are always open to them.

I remember Mike, a senior United Nations Consultant who traveled the world presenting projects. His success depended on his high-level contacts. Twice I saw him pick up a phone and call the president of a country. How did he do it? He called his assistant. Greeted her or him by name and asked questions about their children. And he would remember a story that they had told him on a previous occasion when he had the opportunity to be received by the President. And when he asked to speak to the President, the assistant would say "***Of course, one second... Mr. President, Mike is calling!***

Me, I couldn't remember the name of the President!

3. Learn to analyze other people. It is essential to always consider what kind of person you have before you. If for example we are faced with people who talk a lot, we can be a little freer to express ourselves. But if they don't speak, we must limit ourselves to the topics being discussed. If somebody is *tight,* we can offend or insult them with a casual joke.

My wife has always had the gift of people watching: she can get a reading, a first impression, which is usually right. B**y their fruits** ye shall know them: people are more than words. You can try to sell yourself as refined, and be an expert in protocol, but it only works for short-term relationships.

In long-term relationships, you will reveal what kind of person you really are. Some may cause a positive first impression but in the second, the true personality will come afloat. They will treat waiters badly or will prove to be resentful or egocentric people who prefer to talk rather than listen; or people that wait for anything to feel *attacked*.

In the end, we express who we are. As much as the words say one thing, we end up getting to know others by their actions. A gossip is discovered because he will discuss the lives of all; so will *"the critic"*. The resentful always find others staring *ugly* at him. The negative will always have a bitter face. The lazy, will even have problems to walk. The unpunctual will think it is okay to make others wait.

Discipline is reflected even in the way you eat, or exercise, or how dirty is your car. (My wife just told me this one. I think she is trying to say something). Sooner or later, your personality will emerge. There is nothing hidden under the sun. So beware. If you post on Facebook your drunken parties, and then go looking for a job or a partner, people will notice.

A quick note on conflict. When faced with a conflict, always stay calm. Never raise your voice or make bad gestures. If you offended or hurt another person, apologize. Don't say hurtful things in the heat of an argument. Count to a thousand if necessary. And if you see that you can't reassure the other, leave, so that anger doesn't cause irreparable damage.

PRINCIPLES OF THE CHAPTER

•When words are many, so are the mistakes. Loose lips sink ships (and companies!) Don't tell everyone everything! If you tell your problems to people who objectively can't help, what benefit do you expect? Maybe that they say *"poor you"* and pad you in the back? And only few people will be truly happy with your success and motivate you to keep going. Most, even if they smile at you, will feel envy.

• Entrepreneurs must learn to communicate and express well in public and never lose sight of that nonverbal 90%. Gestures, tone, actions, the nonsense we say when the tongue is not connected to the brain, reveal more about us than what we say or pretend to be

• An intelligent person sharpens the senses of observation, to study what others reveal of themselves. This way you can spot good people and bad people; the valuable people -someone who can be a partner or a potential employee; and those from who you need to get away immediately.

• Listening is a virtue. Sometimes we can't solve a problem because we don't even know what it is about. If you listen carefully and analyze the details, you may see solutions that are beyond the casual observer.

• Nearly all great leaders have been excellent communicators who have successfully sold their ideas. Good communication prevents misunderstandings and reduces the possibility of unpleasant encounters and *free* enemies. *There is no such thing as a small enemy.*

PART FOUR
Skinny Cows, "Situations" And Solutions.

LAW #10.
DON'T LET SITUATIONS DEFEAT YOU

No one knows when his hour will come: as the fish are caught in the net and birds in the trap, so the man, when least expected, is caught in a bad moment. Ecclesiastes 9.12

I begin this chapter with a warning: if you have no problems, if things are going well, and if the advice you have received so far is what you needed to be better entrepreneur, stop reading and go to Chapter Twelve *immediately...*

Moreover, as of this moment, in this book the word *probl3#$* is forbidden, it is considered a bad word, and censored. It is so associated with pain, the negative, our darkest moments... So we should mention it as little as possible, because even the sound is negative.

Words are energy and have tremendous power!

My biggest fear and the last thing you want is to start thinking in negative or *charge* yourself with thoughts of defeat. We are what we think, and according to the famous law of attraction which we have heard so much, we attract what we focus on. So I don't want to cause you to attract... *situations* ... Let's call them *situations*.

Wallace Wattles say that if you want to get out of poverty, stop thinking about poverty and begin thinking about wealth. Same with your *situations*.

My wife says that much of the reason for our *situations*, was that we began to believe those who told us that we were in the midst of them.

The same happened with the global recession. When everyone believes there is a crisis, and that you should not spend or invest because everything is going to be bad, there is no doubt that the collective attitudes cause just that. So all gets worse!

On the contrary I know three close people who never let themselves be convinced that there was a crisis, and surprisingly, the crisis passed them long ... and they all were in real estate, the sector most beaten!

Rather than a crisis these friends saw opportunities, continued to work even harder when others crossed their arms to mourn, and had very good years!

Even one of them who did not get the financial results he expected, keeps telling me: *"I learned and strengthened my character so much, and amended so many mistakes I was making, that now I feel like a lion out of the cage wanting to devour the world and do business like never before"*

Now that years have started to pass, I see him devouring the market, and doing better than before!

Now, warnings made, and knowing that those who read on have been "attacked" by those evil drones we call "situations", let us together learn how to deal with them to become extraordinary entrepreneurs.

a. Some cows lose weight during the winter...

In business, there are good times and bad times. There is the spring and there is the winter. Fat cows, skinny cows, or moments with no cows! And worst, times when we are like the cows, so tired that we are unable to think, and we just ruminate and ruminate...

Sometimes it is our fault (because we have not changed, innovated or followed the market, worked hard enough, or consistently taken care of business).

Other times, external factors aggravate the situation (an economic crisis, a change in the sector in which we operate, a natural disaster), combined with the fact that maybe we don't react as we should...

Bad times come. The night, the storm...One way or another life will test us; test our character with fire.

No matter if you are good or bad, fat or thin, rich or poor, life will __try__ to throw you into the lions' den to see how you react.

I underscored "try" because I am increasingly convinced – moreover after seeing the friends who refused to enter the den and raked until life left them alone, that there is no irrevocable sentence when it comes to suffering.

Now when it comes to dealing with "situations" our enormous ego causes that two positive characteristics take a negative connotation and become mistakes.

The first is to believe we are so special.

This is an excellent feature! If we walk through life believing we are ordinary and deserve nothing special, guess what? Nothing extraordinary will happen to us.

Its downside is that it can make us feel invincible and become careless, so we don't do what we have to do when we have to do it.

The second is to be optimistic.

We see the glass half full and always the bright side. We expect to see gains and never a possible loss. It is also an excellent feature that allows us to take risk; to get into the water and just swim!

But misunderstanding optimism can lead us to ignore principles, to stop being as boy scouts, *always ready!* So when the bad times arrive we are taken by surprise! Sometimes we even see the writing on the wall, we smell the beast from far, but we refuse to cry *"wolf"* ... until it is biting our neck !

In this book I wanted to convey that to succeed in business, you must be prepared, save, have good employees and partners, be intelligently suspicious, not to jump after anything that looks like an opportunity, understand the importance of cash and reserves, etc.

I made clear that the difference between successfully navigate the waves of a tumultuous sea, or be wallowing on the reef in pieces, is **preparation**, is in doing things right, and in understanding that success is in our hands.

Now, let's assume that despite everything, despite kicking and punching the monster, the storm caught you with no umbrella or you were thrown into the lion's den...

The following example, which analyzes a bad handling of situations that led an entrepreneur from success to failure, can help -by showing you a mirror, so that learning from the mistakes of others, can get you out of your own without much suffering. Something I've learned over the years is that:

When you are in the lion's den, as you hear the roar of those big cats approaching, you must understand that whatever you are going through, many -perhaps thousands, have already lived it at some point or another.

Or do you really believe you are the only one who has had good years, fortune has smiled you and blessed you with money, to the point of thinking that you are at the top?

Or the only one with situations so huge that seems to have no end?

Or with unfaithful employees, ungrateful customers or a bit of bad luck?

Why is it so important to understand this?

First, because sometimes we can find in the stories of others, solutions to our situations.

Secondly, by seeing the mistakes others have made in our position -if we are alert and pay attention, we can have better prospects and perhaps take a different route.

Thirdly, because at least to know that we are not alone -that others have been through it- can help us keep our self-esteem, which usually ends hardest hit after a storm...

b. A short time ago, in a galaxy close, close by...

This is the story of a character whose only connection to Star Wars was that he actually believed *he was a star!*

The story is important because his mistakes represent the daily drama of thousands of entrepreneurs worldwide. Because whether in China, Chile, Germany, United States or Costa Rica, we entrepreneurs are all the same!

It is also an example of an incorrect application -or lack of application of the principles of this book.

Our character, who had made millions in successful businesses, began living under the pretense that he had infinite resources: the image that in his pride had sold to everyone, including himself. And then, he began to make mistakes...

First mistake. He was ashamed of collecting what was owed to him and began to give concessions to customers based in 'pride'. Debtors went to him thinking *"he has too much money anyway",* and told him they couldn't make the payments. He, with false pride, said it didn't matter. *"Okay. Pay me later. You are good people. I can give you time."*

This error also stemmed from something I mentioned before: customers had made him believe they were his friends. He had been invited to birthday parties. He could not say no...

Violating this principle led to two consequences.

• Rumors spread, and in the future in similar conditions, all are going to expect similar treatment. If you gave a concession to one, the others expect the same...

• People often confuse kindness with weakness. And from there, things only grow...

Second mistake. His contracts were too 'soft' because he assumed people were good and kept their promises, so, he never foresaw consequences if they breached. And people do breach contracts! People forget commitments! Remember STA - Selective Temporary Amnesia... What? Don't tell me you already forgot the principle of doing good contracts...

Third mistake. He was so busy and dispersed in his various companies (remember one has limited time and energy) and perhaps, at the end, he had gotten lazy, that the idea of suing those who didn't pay was so unappealing, that he didn't! Once again, rumors spread. And this is time for another truth:

If you let someone wrong you, and you don't defend yourself, it sends the message that you are weak and don't know how or can't protect yourself. It shows that you are fair game, and given the right circumstances, most people can become predators without mercy.

These mistakes generated financial shortcomings. And in trying to deal with them (he didn't have a cash reserve for bad times or foolish decisions), he made even more serious mistakes.

Fourth mistake. He got *high interest* loans, full of fees and expenses, for it seemed easier than to be tough with his clients, easier than to collect from his *'friends'*, or sue based on his soft contracts. To do this, he mortgaged his assets for pennies on the dollar, sure that luck would follow him and soon everything would be fine and he could repay. And since the assets were really good, he was never short of 'friends' who would lend him money, already suspecting he was not going to be able to repay.

Time went on and more and more frequently he had to deal with creditors. As they expected to be paid the interest on time - and he wanted to protect his reputation, he made the **Fifth mistake:** He began to pay interests with the little working capital he had. After a while, everything was going to interests, and very little to build houses.

He either paid the interests or worked.

And since saving his reputation was still his silly obsession, he paid the interests. He never tried to renegotiate: "Look, if I pay now, I will not be able to generate money for next month payment" *'Shame on you!'* He imagined they would say. *'Is the tycoon in trouble?'*

How could he ask a favor, understanding or time? Sure they would say no and give him an ugly look. Perhaps they would tell other people he was not as cool and *'fabulous'* as, in his mind, everybody thought he was.

So what did he do? He continued to pay interests, and gradually ran out of money to work and properties to mortgage...

And this is where he made his **sixth mistake.** The fatal one. When things were getting out of control he got scared, his mind blocked, and he just sat down to wait for a miracle. He began to expect for something supernatural. Instead of working even harder; of thinking of solutions, he began to "visualize" someone with a lot of money buying his business or offering to be his partner; or to visualize him winning the lottery... After all, he deserved it, right? He was a good guy, had worked hard...

Some have that stroke of luck, and good for them. But for most it is probably not going to be as easy.

To our *fabulous* entrepreneur the miracle didn't arrive. And because he did not seek for solutions in time, trying to save first his reputation -he ended up losing millions and the work of his life.

You have to learn to act in time.

You can't wait until you fall so deep in trouble that only a miracle can save you.

c. Save your *behind*, then save face.

This case -and his obsession to save the reputation, is very common and understandable, especially with honest people who have used their lives in order to build a name and a position. Reputation is important and should be protected.

However, I once met a billionaire, a real estate entrepreneur from Canada, who was interested in buying one of my projects. With his vast experience, he studied my business with a depth that I had never seen (accountants and assistants flew to Costa Rica, and studied for a week everything. And I mean EVERYTHING!) With that level of analysis, he saw things that I haven't (years earlier!), and made me an offer which at that time I thought was very low, but now I know it was completely realistic. I, *of course*, refused.

I was so clever, a hare, remember? I was sure I could do better by myself. And the situations that he claimed to have found, I attributed them to the fact that the shark wanted my buildings for little money... Yeah, right! I should have accepted! After years of suffering and losing, I realized that everything he had said was true!

However, this section is not about that business, but about the principle that billionaire taught me, which I will always remember because it is so true. I can almost hear him saying:

"Mauricio, save your ass!

Then, only then, start thinking about saving your pretty face! (I added *pretty*).

If you do the opposite, you end up losing both. "

Sometimes things do not go our way ... But since we have such a high concept of ourselves because we may have been successful for years, it gives us a huge shame that others know that we are entangled and that our grass is not as green as people thought.

Then, to save the reputation becomes the ultimate goal in times of trouble. But always remember:

First, save your 'behind'. Trying to save face (reputation), at the expense of whatever... can be the final nail to hang us in the wall of failure.

We all have heard of an entrepreneur that has this principle very clear: Donald Trump.

He has filed for bankruptcy in several of his companies. However, do you see him in the press embarrassed, calling himself a failure and promising not to do it again? NO! What you probably see is the ad for another TV show in which he will teach the contestants how to be good entrepreneurs. Trump has realized that you can't win all the time, but mostly, that you are not expected to win them all. And so, he has been able to navigate virtually untouched the chapter 11's, conserving capital to keep going. Because by recognizing situations that require tough decisions; and by acting on time even if it represents a little damage to his reputation, he has been able to save what is worth saving and move on.

d. Some advice on debt.

Lack of money and debt are the number one cause for us not sleeping at night. Here are some tips for those who are experiencing financial situations:

1. To pay or not to pay. Although I don't promote easy ways out, as a golden rule, you should stop paying your creditors when that money is what you absolutely need to produce, to generate. You have to buy supplies to keep producing and generating new business or your company WILL DISAPPEAR!

Do you remember the story of the goose that lays the golden eggs?

You can pay with so many golden eggs as you want.

However, never, never, never give up the goose.

Do that and you are lost!

If you can't produce, if you can't build, if you can't generate revenue...

How will you pay your debts?

'But if I default with my creditors, I will never get loans again!'

It's a possibility, but now you need to solve more urgent and immediate issues. If you take action in time, you may eventually be able to pay them all. And the only interest of creditors is to be paid. If they see your effort and you end up paying, they will lend you again. But talk to them, they need to know why you are doing it. It is important to face your situations.

So, the rule is, no matter what, stop payment on your creditors the moment that payment is not the normal payment produced by your company, but when it is the very money you are using to produce, to generate.

2. To lose or not to lose. Analyze mortgage backed debts. Are the interests killing you? People have a lot of trouble accepting the principle that sometimes losing is winning, and that by losing something in the long run they may be winning.

Sometimes we hold an asset paying high interests for years, waiting for a miracle, and we have to run every month to get the money to pay, mortgaging other things to keep up... And we end up losing the original asset ... and everything else!

Besides, if you add the capital, plus all interest paid, multiplied by all the time you failed to produce because you were thinking about it instead of working, raised to the square root of life lost and stress accumulated...

The money can be recovered, or made again, perhaps in even larger quantities. But your time, your energy, your life ... They never return. It is cheaper to let go of certain things, losing them this time, reorganize, breath, start again with a firm foundation, make money again, and buy them back just to show destiny!

And under no circumstances ask for loans to pay off other loans to pay off other loans ... I know what it is to see a debt of $40,000 becoming $100,000, and going from possibly losing one lot to lose two houses, all for pride and not letting it go.

Learn another truth:

Sometimes you win, sometimes you lose.

Nobody expects you to always win.

The important thing is that you keep your sanity and the ability to work. Anything you lose, if you love it that much, you can buy it back when you have recovered. There is a 50% chance that the market goes down and you even can buy it back cheaper in the future; or maybe you do so well that that money is nothing to you.

3. To sell or not to sell. Do you have a property that you love dearly, but can make you some cash? Sell it! We said that after you can buy it back if you want, but you need the cash flow NOW! However, don't sell your property unless you have taken steps so that money will pull you out of the mess. Do not keep pouring water into a bucket that has holes everywhere. First, cover the holes; or in six months, you will be exactly in the same place, but without the property!

4. To fire or not to fire. Analyze your payroll. Do you have unproductive employees that you can't put to work immediately? Or employees that are not producing because of all the problems, but when things improve you would want to be with you? Almost always is better to let them go, and explain them. If you save yourself, and if you took the tough decisions, it may be possible to rehire them later. BUT use common sense. Obviously do not dismiss those vital to your business, or the cure may be worse than the disease.

5. To close or not to close. Analyze your ways out. Do you have to close a shop that losses money every month? Do you have to reduce its hours?

In 2002, after tourism receded due to September 11, I had to close a hotel that lost $5,000 a month. It was the first time I got involved in a lot of business at a time (and I did not learn my lesson!).

My wife said "close it, let it go..." But I said: NEVER! Ten months and $50,000 in losses later, I listened to her. I closed it and ... nothing happened!

Today I barely remember the infamous hotel (I remembered it to write this example). But how much I suffered to let it go! And every month I suffered losing $5,000! I thank my wife, for after everything happened, she never said "I told you so" or comment on my stubbornness.

Donald Trump says that *"part of being a winner is knowing when enough is enough. Sometimes you have to give up the fight and walk away, and move on to something that is more productive."*

6. To seek or not to seek legal protection. If you have studied the situation from every angle and it is at a point which is too complicated, there are always protection laws, like chapter 11 bankruptcy. These provisions are there to help when you can't do it by yourself. The big ones are big because they know when to ask for help... Remember General Motors, Chrysler and Trump, many, many, many times (which means he is not such a winner after all. But, that is politics...)

e. You look nicer with your mouth SHUT!

Nobody has to know what it going on! Nor your employees, nor your family (except your spouse), your 'friends' or your neighbors, let alone the bartender or the waiter at the restaurant. Don't place yourself in everybody's conversation!

Even in the midst of situations and even if many people already know, don't walk around telling everyone! If you have to lose a property, close a store, or fire someone, do it! BUT BE DISCREET!

By our lack of discretion, we cause ourselves some serious problems! Why? Because if people realize that we are not doing so well, even a creditor whose term was not up will find a reason to request payment. And the last thing we need is more pressure.

It requires a lot of discipline to not *air* our situations with the friend we found at the supermarket. *"Oh, man, things are tough, cash flow has been hard, sales are weak. The situation is bad for everyone, you know!"*

DON'T DO IT! What will you gain? Nothing... but ... No! Nothing! And what will you lose? You still don't have a clue! But sooner than later, you will find out. How? When another creditor knock at your door...

Because, and it happens, the friend you just told will tell somebody else, especially if you are well known. Human beings, we enjoy talking about other people's problems. It makes us feel more 'equal', especially if we are in trouble ourselves. And the world, your country, your city, and especially your inner circle are extraordinarily small. And that innocent remark can become the confirmation for your supplier to no longer sell you on credit; or the red light your banker needed for not drawing the approved credit line; or the confirmation your client needed to seek a new supplier, because you are in danger of becoming 'unreliable'.

So, shut up!

If asked directly, brush it off, smile, and say that all is well. If they know you are limping, do not confirm it. If possible, convince them otherwise.

Once, an acquaintance was in financial 'situations' (by the way, hard to believe since he is now so wealthy. That confirms we all have downs, and UPs!). He made the mistake of allowing a few people to know about it, and the rumors started.

Then he had an idea a bit strange.

With his last dollars he bought a used Mercedes -that looked new, and went on to drive it everywhere. He would go to meetings and made sure everybody see him. And when asked *'but weren't you in trouble?'* he would reply, smiling *'What? 'No! That was a rumor I started to negotiate better terms with the bank!'*

And it worked. People continued doing business with him, convinced it was all a clever rumor.

The truth is, when people confirm that you are out of money, many will run from you: they want to be as far as possible from the "bad luck".

If you represent that at one point, they flee as if you are the worst of the lepers.

Unfortunately not only false friends, but -and that's the worst-, customers, suppliers and bankers.

And now more than ever, you need people who want to do business with you...

PRINCIPLES OF THE CHAPTER

• In business there are good times and bad times. Sometimes, the bad times are our fault (we didn't change, innovate or work hard enough). And a crisis or natural factors could contribute to aggravate the situation.

• If the storm found you without umbrella, remember that a negative attitude only brings more difficulties. A positive attitude, or at least neutral attitude of calm, will allow you to reflect and think about solutions.

• Bad times can have a positive effect. They are the best way to learn the lessons, grow and gain strength. If they arrive at your door, remember, it already happened to someone, so you can search history on how it went, or what mistakes that character made.

• Your reputation is important. But sometimes trying to save it at all cost, can become the final nail to hang us in the wall of failure. First save your ass. Then worry about saving face. If you lose the first one, definitely will also lose the second.

• Don't tell your situation to everyone. Most can't help you and what they will do is to comment with others behind their backs. And you don't know if the other was the banker who was about to give you a loan, and because of your loud mouth, it all fell apart!

• If your "situation" is a debt that is consuming you, and you are beginning to use working capital to keep 'current while awaiting a miracle, you are making a big mistake.

Stop paying your creditors if you are using the money you need to work. If you stop producing, you may pay this month, but the next will be the same or worse. But please explain your creditors (and don't let them persuade you on how important is *to keep your reputation*). In the end, if you get out of trouble and pay them, they will lend you again

• You need your employees to produce, and you have to pay their wages. Have you ever had employees without pay, muttering defeated, waiting for the company to close and for somebody to tell them that is the last check? Because, don't be fooled, they think this from the first time you don't pay them on time, even if in your mind you believe the problem is minor and temporary ! Or maybe they have their wages, but no tools or supplies because there is no money for supplies or advertisement to generate new customers

• Workers know what you refuse to accept: they are experts in reading the writing on the wall. They see your face and know about your sleepless night. Sometimes they see the picture clearer than you, because they are not waiting for the miracle. They are waiting for a check and in the meantime, they are looking for another job. And you can't blame them, their job is their only source of income. They have no savings, have debts and a family to feed. So can you blame them if you are not the only concern in their minds?

• If you have to let go of an employee because you can't pay the wages, if you have to close a business, or let loose a property, because the mortgage are killing you, do it! Sometimes we postpone the inevitable, and on the way, we lose more and more. It's like quicksand: the more we try to get out, the more we go down. Losing something, in the long run, may be winning. We lose life, stress, other assets, trying to save it, rather than continue producing or looking for new opportunities that allow us to someday buy back that we lost (if we miss it so much!) . Conrad Hilton, founder of Hilton Hotels, lost his hotels during the depression of 1929. Despite this setback he continued working as an administrator, until he could repurchase them.

• Even before a failure, never forget that almost all the greatest entrepreneurs in history -as Hilton, lost their fortunes one or more times. It's like pruning a plant : to grow even stronger, we should remove excess leaves . Life use these scissors (and if you are the plant, it hurts!) to remove everything that has been striking. It is a way perhaps cruel to eliminate insects that suck the sap (sound familiar?). Vices, mistakes, excess baggage... But remember that the most important of a plant is its stem, its heart. While the stem is alive, the plant is alive. And you can regrow even larger than before.

LAW #11

CONCENTRATE ON SOLUTIONS.

a. Stop, Think, Regroup

We said that you have to learn to act in time. And to do that, the formula begins by having the strength and character to take timely decisions, no matter how inconvenient or hard they are.

When you are in the midst of a difficult situation (and I hope you never do) or if you encounter a rainy day (which are generally also dark!), the first advice I can give you, (so hopefully you face them without getting gored) is: STOP AND THINK!

It's okay to fight, kick, bite and pinch... But know when to stop to take a breath and see how effective you are being. Sometimes we are so busy pinching, that we don't realize that we have been hitting the monster in the shell. Maybe when we stop and analyze, we can find the little hole where we are supposed to attack...

Find some peace, sit down and think.

In the midst of the storm, or feeling the heat of the fire, or in the lions' den, you can't think because you are obsessed with surviving.

Not only you don't think clearly, but don't work enough, don't sleep enough, don't believe, don't innovate, don't see the opportunities and at times, don't recognize miracles.

Don't forget that it was your vision and creativity which led you to great things, and so you have to find a way to reconnect with it, even if it appears that you are free falling and your face is about to hit the floor.

So, stay calm. Don't panic. Stop paddling desperately trying to get out of the storm. Stop trying to open the oven out of the fire.

Stop!

Now, take a deep breath, and as mentioned in the previous chapter, prepare to reorganize your life and your business, because probably there is something you are doing wrong! Perhaps the miracle that positive thinkers await could be just the opportunity to sit down, analyze everything, and discover in time what to do to save your business.

Here, I'm going to let you cry a little. I know it hurts. I cried a lot myself! But know that when the tears are gone, you have to get to work. For maybe the miracle is that eventually, in a demonstration of your character, you make the decisions you need no matter how hard they are.

Your ability to survive the difficulties is directly proportional to your ability to stop, think and make decisions regardless of what others will think or if your friends are going to laugh at you and whisper that you are a failure. Because if you don't take the hard decisions, and keep doing what you're doing, they are going to laugh anyway...

b. Focus your talents and energy on the solutions

I know what you're thinking. Easy to say but hard to do. If only I knew what you are going through, right? Believe me, I know more than you think. I won't tell you my story -we would cry together, but I'll give you a piece of advice:

No matter how many situations you are facing, if you just think about them, you will not get anywhere.

It will paralyze you; and the paralysis only brings more complications, because you attract what you think.

Instead of remaining paralyzed; focus each morning in finding at least ONE solution. When I talk about situations, I talk about the large ones, those that require your full attention and strength. Little emergencies arise all the time and we tend to deceive ourselves solving those, and never dealing with the real issues.

"I can't, I have no time..." You know that's false. Stop playing in the computer, sit down and think. It's scary, I know. It's sad, I know. You feel anger, because usually it all started because of a mistake or a bad decision we made, and we shouldn't have. *If I don't think about it may disappear...'*

No!

'Then?'

Then, take a sheet of paper. Write it down. You would get the chills just by writing it. But there it is. It is real and will not go unless you defeat it. And to do it, you have to write every possible solution that comes to mind.

Do you have to call someone and ask a favor, but you ashamed? Write it down.

Do you have to call the lawyer and ask him to start the law suit? Write it down.

Do you have to call and tell your client you can't deliver the product? Write it down.

Do you have to call the creditor, ask for more time, and explain the situation instead of hiding? Write it down.

And throughout this process, block the negative thoughts. You can only think of one thing at a time. If they are positive things, you can't think of anything negative. Negative thoughts will fight back, as screens "pop - ups" of Windows. It is in you put the filter and stay positive.

Do not lose sight that even the patriarchs in the Bible faced seemingly intractable situations. Abraham, Isaac, Jacob, and Moses, despite talking to God, went through periods of drought and despair.

Modern Patriarchs as Steve Jobs slept in hallways, having nothing to eat... Nelson Mandela was imprisoned, tortured and waiting for death for twenty YEARS.

But if they were able to beat the great drought, why are you still saying you can't?

Stop issuing negative commands to your brain, and get to find solutions. If you really locked yourself in your office, turned off the phone, and concentrate all your energies, something will happen; an answer will show up. If you can't find the magical solution, at least it will clarify the picture, and hopefully, you will realize is not that terrible after all.

I'm sure after making a list of solutions, some will seem impossible, others almost "miraculous", but maybe you think of something you have not thought before. And why not? Because you were concentrated in the negative!

Difficulties have a negative charge; and while you are stressed, with gastritis and feeling it is the end of the world, solutions -which are positively charged, cannot approach a negatively charged mind. It is a principle of quantum physics.

But if the charge is at least neutral (i.e. somehow you place yourself above your difficulties for a while) the solutions may appear.

I challenge you right now to take a sheet of paper. What is the worst thing that you are facing?

What doesn't let you sleep, or be happy, or smile to your children when they seek for your attention.

Write it down in detail. With your own hand. Tell the story...

Then, as soon as you finish reading these instructions, close your eyes and visualize a positive memory, a positive moment. Remember that time when fortune smiled and you were very successful?

Or that happy moment in your past that you still remember and it still makes you smile?

Mine is when my daughter was born and I had her in my arms for the first time... How happy I was!

Relive those moments... Breathe deeply. If you want, pray a little and ask for guidance (or if you believe you can do it by yourself, it is okay too).

And now that you are in a positive frequency, call the solutions, think of solutions, write down everything that comes to mind.

Stop reading. Do this now!

PRINCIPLES OF THE CHAPTER

• Your ability to survive is directly proportional to your ability to stop, think and make decisions no matter what. In the center of the storm, neither you nor anyone else can think, because you are obsessed with survival. Then, you don't work hard enough, don't get enough sleep, don't create, don't innovate, don't see the opportunities and sometimes don't even recognize the miracles knocking at your door.

Dale Carnegie suggests the following rules to defeat worry:

"When you, or any of your associates are tempted to worry about a problem, write out and answer the following questions:

a. What is the problem?

b. What is the cause of the problem?

c. What are all possible solutions?

d. What is the best solution?"

Therefore, do not wait until you fall so deep in trouble that only a miracle can save you. Act in time. Once you have your list of possible solutions, Take Action! Make the calls. Seek for the help you need. Ask for the advice you have to ask. But do it. Sleeping late and playing solitaire will just extend the suffering.

• The difference between success and failure in dealing with *situations* is in how we face them, how we prepare for battle. If you think you are going to lose, you will lose: there is no saving you. But if you think you are going to succeed, you will. It is difficult to accept this philosophy that thoughts are things and we are architects of our own destiny by what we think, whether positive or negative. Difficult to accept or not, it is TRUE!

• Bad Luck is a lazy lady. If anyone is resisting hard, she better go and look elsewhere for someone who will accept defeat. There are so many of those anyway!

LAW #12.
SEEK HELP FROM THE INFINITE INTELLIGENCE; BUT BE 'INTELLIGENT' ABOUT IT

"The scientist's religious feeling takes the form of a rapturous amazement at the harmony of natural law, which reveals an intelligence of such superiority that, compared with it, all the systematic thinking and acting of human beings is utterly insignificant reflection." Albert Einstein

I had to think much before including a chapter that mentions God in a business book. I called Him "Infinite Intelligence" because most see the word 'God' in the index, get scared and buy the next book.

People believe that if a book mentions God is probably boring... However, if it mentions 'Energy that Flows', 'Universal Energy', 'Universal Source' 'One Mind', 'Supreme Spirit', 'Supreme Power', 'Infinite Intelligence', 'Nature', 'Substance' or 'Matter', they buy it without problem, convinced that it is full of wisdom ...

It has become so *unfashionable* to talk about God! It's almost socially unacceptable. Those who attain some success, we call ourselves 'modern thinkers'. We believe *'our way'*, and hence, prefer to speak of *Universal Energy*. Talking about God make us think about *religion*. And because we see so many people stuck in it --people who believe they hold the absolute truth and the moral right to demonstrate superiority--, the topic upsets us.

We believe anyone who talks about God just wants to bring us to a temple to sing Hallelujahs; and for ever forget about drinking a little wine, telling a little joke, or dancing a little tight, and therefore, life will become... well, a little *boring*...

And by focusing on these stereotypes, we lose sight of the true meaning of that Supreme Power...

a. Seek God for the right reasons

There are moments in life when, despite everything we know or do, or even if *we focus on success,* we get derailed, *situations* 'attack us', and we fell lonely, desperate and are unable to see a way out.

And because we don't understand that God is much bigger than the stereotypes of the people or places that believe to represent Him, we may turn away from an infinite power that can certainly help us both in bad times, as in good.

I was one of many that during this recent global recession, when I was tired and dejected by the skinny cows, went desperately begging for a quick way out.

I had not being inside a church for ten years and suddenly... I was going every Sunday! and Mondays, and Thursdays, and to Bible study on Friday!

I just wanted God to see *how much I have changed!*

I was one of those who didn't understand that at the time of trial -the vulnerable moments, is when you should be more careful, and seek God for the right reasons.

I have a confession: I did it just to see if God helped me *'quickly', easily and without pain*... but kept thinking that if He didn't help me fast, I would stop believing and going to church...

A serious error which we tend to make when we don't understand the true meaning of approaching God, is to believe that by singing praising songs we have the *'acquired right'* to just sit and wait for a miracle.

And it could be worse yet if we get ourselves a *spiritual guide* who tells us that, since God loves us (and he does, don't get me wrong!), he would get us out of trouble without effort on our part! All we have to do is to **buy** a little miracle from that God appointed representative, *if you know what I mean...*

But although the Supreme can give us an easy out - and I imagine there are those who are given it, it's not what usually happens. I recently heard a warning about this:

Good Luck and miracles can't be bought or sold.

Beware of those who try to sell them

In short, this is a complicated topic! The point is, sometimes we are so desperate we believe everything they say to us, and we just sat down to wait... I know many who have. I myself learned the hard way that that is not how things operate. *I don't want you to make that mistake.*

b. The way out requires work and effort

The great motivator Jim Rohn said, "You are exactly where you deserve to be, and have exactly what you deserve to have. If you don't want to be there, CHANGE!"

If you made mistake after mistake, were reckless, irresponsible and proud (I'm trying to remember what other sins I committed!), and things went wrong, it was DEFINITELY

NOT because God is punishing you. NO. God doesn't like *to punish people*. We seek the results with our actions.

And since your situations **are not** some divine punishment, if you are in *situations*, the only secret to get out is to try to understand what mistakes you made, and make them no more. Jesus explained this when he said to a man he healed "Go and sin no more", which was saying: "If you keep doing the same, the same will happen again."

Yes, it's good to communicate with God -the Source of All Things. It's good independently of business. As a human being you grow and improve. Those are the right reasons. And I have no doubt that if you look for God, if you ask for help the Infinite Force will respond.

But, although I know God can do it, don't expect a check in the mail! Or immediate results, something like *"I pray in the morning, and it is all solved in the afternoon!"*

Faith will not save you from problems immediately; but it will help you navigate without sinking. And if it is part of HIS plan, HE will illuminate the ideas and opportunities, or will put you on the road to the right people. No matter what is happening or how serious the issue in which you are stuck, nothing lasts forever and as bad as that year, or two, or five seems, it will too pass and one day be only a bad memory. Or a good one, if you learned the lessons and grew stronger.

If despite everything I've said, you insist on seeking God only when in trouble, as the majority do (and again, I am including myself on this group), let me remind you that you should not expect Him to do the work for you or to solve your company's problems for you. To confront creditors or to restructure your debt. To improve your marketing; adjust your costs; make the calls; get better suppliers; dismiss employees who are stealing or get rid of the bad partner you chose. All while you're in church, praying...

They say God *'feeds the birds of the field'*. *Some* think this is an example of *why work so hard?* The reality is the bird goes early to work to seek the worm, as my friend Eric told me once:

Worms don't rain from the sky. Nor solutions. The worst thing you can do is to act defeated and let your hopes and dreams slip away, or just lie on a bed praying for a miracle.

It doesn't work like that! God, already made perfect since inception and put within you ALL you need.

HE will help, will give you strength, and occasionally, a miracle, so you know he is there observing and you are not alone and helpless. But you have to do the working!

My daughter Maria José, with her rare wisdom, told me this example when she was seven:

"God gives us the hammer and nails.

But we have to get to the wall, lift the nail, use the hammer, and nail it!"

Do not make the mistake of looking to God to get you out of those situations you got yourself in. Look to him for peace, calm, ideas, inspiration and wisdom, so you, with that ability He gave you, will find answers and solutions. Because there are; and if you put yourself in action and focus, you will find them.

And there, my friends, lies the real miracle.

So why wait to be in the midst of difficulties?

I don't pretend to own the absolute truth nor I cry to have received a "revelation", just want you to remember that this Force, or God if you prefer, is the infinite intelligence that inspires and gives clarity, and if you are willing to be guided - and willing to do your part, the solutions will come.

PRINCIPLES OF THE CHAPTER

• 90% of people believe that God is important in their lives. 72% says it is important in business. Don't be ashamed or afraid of seeking His help.

• If you are facing difficult situations, don't be fooled by those who tell you to pray a little; *buy* a little miracle (from them), sit down and wait, and everything will resolve. If you remain in the sofa, even if you pray all day, problems won't get smaller nor disappear. They will continue to grow a bit each day. If you face them early, they may be small; but if you wait...

• Seek God because it will bring peace, and that peace will make you more efficient in the search for an exit from your personal labyrinth. But any exit, any solution, any ideas, require effort. God will enlighten you with ideas, will put the right people in your way or will bring you opportunities, but is in you to maximize them.

• Everything is easier if you know something bigger than you is by your side. My wife and I pray, ask a question or request guidance, and open the Bible in the first place we feel. And we receive incredible answers!

• Seeking God's help doesn't mean living in penitence or losing a bit of your essence. Keep smiling, dancing, and telling jokes. Being happy improves your health and the possibility for fresh ideas. And those fresh ideas are the ones who will allow you to become one of those great and successful entrepreneurs.

THE END

www.ingramcontent.com/pod-product-compliance
Lightning Source LLC
Chambersburg PA
CBHW070246190526
45169CB00001B/321